JimHole LoisHole

volume 3

perennials

Practical Advice and the
Science Behind It

H
HOLE'S
ENJOY GARDENING

PUBLISHED BY HOLE'S
101 Bellerose Drive
St. Albert, Alberta Canada
T8N 8N8

Printed in Canada   5   4   3   2

Canadian Cataloguing in Publication Data

Hole, Lois, 1933–
  Perennials

(Questions & answers ; 3)
Includes index.
ISBN 0-9682791-7-1

  1. Perennials. I. Hole, Jim, 1956- II. Title. III. Series: Questions & answers (St. Albert, Alta.) ; 3.
SB434.H643 2000   635.9'32   C00-910315-5

Colour separations and film by Elite Lithographers, Edmonton, Alberta, Canada
Printed and bound by Friesens, Altona, Manitoba, Canada.

Contents

Acknowledgements

Thanks to our perennials experts Bob Stadnyk, Jan Goodall, all the members of the perennials department, and Dorothy Jedrasik. Your passion and experience have been indispensable in the preparation of this book.

Thanks also to our other staff members, who recorded all the questions found in this book during some very busy times.

Finally, thanks to all of the perennial enthusiasts, new and old, who took the time to ask questions. Your curiosity has helped us make many new and valuable discoveries.

The *Q&A* Series—
Practical Advice
and the Science Behind It

Perennials ❧ Practical Advice and the Science Behind It completes the first trilogy of our new *Q&A* series. While many of the most common questions are covered in *Bedding Plants*, *Roses*, and this volume, there is still plenty of ground to cover, across a wide range of home and garden topics. *Vegetables* and *Trees & Shrubs* are on the horizon; future volumes may answer questions on pests and disease, landscaping, and a variety of other topics, all by the appropriate experts.

Success is built on a solid foundation of questions. Every innovation comes about because someone asked, "How does this process work? And how can I make it work better?" A good question can open up whole new worlds—new ways of doing things, new perspectives, and new information about secrets once hidden.

That information is what good gardening is all about. Our goal has always been to provide gardeners, no matter what their skill level, with the information they need to grow beautiful plants—and to accomplish this in the most enjoyable manner. Accordingly, different people want different kinds of information. We've answered the questions in two parts: a short answer for those who are eager to solve a problem and get back to their projects, and a more in-depth answer for those who want to spend a little time learning what makes their favourite hobby tick. In short, we deliver practical advice and the science behind it.

At Hole's, we've always tried to ask the right questions, and to listen carefully when they come from someone else. The questions in the *Q&A* books didn't spring from our heads—they were collected from hundreds of people, from coast to coast. Over the past dozen years, we've been recording the best questions we've run across, from the simple questions we thought beginning gardeners could identify with to the head-scratchers that gave us pause. The inquiries came from walk-in customers, letters, phone calls, and e-mails. Some came from audiences during one or another of our radio or television appearances; others from the folks we've spoken to at gardening talks all across the continent. A few came from our own employees during the day-to-day operations of our greenhouse. No matter what the source, each inquiry contained within itself a valuable piece of information: it told us what people wanted to know, and gave us a guide with which to build this series of books.

Answering these questions has been as valuable for us as for the questioners. They've pushed us to the limits of our knowledge, urging us to dig deeper for the truth.

Lois Hole and Jim Hole
July 2000

Introduction
by Lois Hole

My son Jim and I, along with the rest of the family, have been interested in perennials for many years now. Their diverse beauty captures our imagination, and we expect many gardeners feel the same way. While we've enjoyed perennials in our home gardens for decades, our professional involvement with perennials took several years to come into full flower—much like the plants themselves. In many ways, the story of perennials at Hole's Greenhouses & Gardens is the story of Bob Stadnyk, the man who manages and largely created our perennials department. We have learned a lot in the relatively brief period since our perennials department was formed; our collective knowledge of perennials has grown through a lengthy process of trial and error, sometimes frustrating, sometimes absurd, but ultimately very rewarding.

In the Beginning

We didn't start selling perennials until the mid 1980s, when one member of the family—I'm pretty sure it was my daughter-in-law, Valerie—said simply, "Hey, we should have some perennials." So we asked Dorothy Jedrasik, one of Valerie's helpers in the bedding-plant department, to order a few. Well, Dorothy ordered about 30 or 40 plants and they did quite well—it seems that the more we offered, the more people wanted to try new things. The amount of information to keep track of quickly became almost overwhelming, so Dorothy put together a rudimentary perennial manual, a guidebook for the staff that included care tips for all of the perennials that we were carrying. It wasn't fancy, but it did the job, and, like all good information, saved the staff and customers a lot of time and headaches.

Eventually the demand for perennials grew so much that Dorothy recommended we create an official perennials department and devote some space and personnel to the task. But we didn't really know anyone with more than basic knowledge about perennials—or so we thought.

Bob to the Rescue

My son Bill and Dave Grice faced the difficult task of appointing someone to develop a whole new department. After some discussion, Dave tentatively suggested a young man named Bob Stadnyk, who'd been watering for us for some time and had often worked with Dorothy. "I don't know how much he really knows about perennials, though," Dave said. Bob was, and remains, a quiet type—he did nothing to promote himself. But Bob had developed a rapport with my husband Ted, and Dorothy had good things to say about him, too. So it wasn't as if Dave and Bill were just flipping a coin and seeing what happened (although Bob likes to make jokes to that effect).

Fortunately, we soon discovered that although he was new to the garden-centre business, Bob had grown up with perennials and was really quite an expert. Bob was passionate about perennials, in his words, from "day one," reading about them, visiting garden centres, and searching, often in vain, for the exotic plants he found in old library books. "Oddly enough, I'd often find the rarest stuff in old run-down places," Bob laughs, "but the hunt was part of the fun. There's nothing like the rush you get when you manage to get your hands on a rare perennial that hardly anyone else knows about."

Bob tackled the job with gusto. He knew that information was absolutely crucial to success, so Bob made the revision and updating of our home-made perennial guide one of his first tasks. Then he placed his first order of perennials, bringing in around 400 different varieties, many more than Dorothy's early orders.

"Am I doing this right?" Bob would ask me in those early days. "You just go ahead and handle things however you feel is best," I told him.

My confidence wasn't misplaced. Once again, the more varieties we offered, the more people grew accustomed to experimenting with new perennials, many of them quite exotic by Canadian standards. Just a few years later, Bob's experience with these different varieties was a great help to me when I wrote *Perennial Favorites*. It's since become the bestselling gardening book in Canada.

Higher Learning

Learning about perennials is one of our passions, but sometimes the task involves unexpected hazards.

Perennials Manager, Bob Stadnyk

Bob has a great story about his pre-Hole's days. "I was up in Athabasca, helping my boss at the time to divide some valerian. This was my first experience with the plant, but everything seemed to be going fine. We had to pick up some tiger-lily seed in the middle of the job, so we left the plants in the shade of my boss' house and drove off in his little Toyota. When we returned, we were greeted by a stumbling horde of the boss' cats, who had gotten completely squirrelly on the valerian—as it turns out, the stuff is worse than catnip. The driveway was full of dazed felines, and just as we were pulling in, the car's brakes went out. The cats were oblivious to my boss' frantic honking, so we wound up driving into the bushes to avoid a catastrophe. If you have pets, here's a lesson—don't leave halluci-nogenic plants lying around!"

More recently, the perennials department played host to pink Lady's Slippers for the first time. Bob had heard that these Lady's Slippers needed a certain fungus in the soil to grow properly, so he asked a friend at the Devonian Botanic Gardens to cultivate a batch of the fungus for him. Soon the fungus was ready, and Bob added it to the ladyslippers' soil. However, Bob had been given the wrong information—and the results were mildly horrific, for the fungus not only killed the Lady's Slippers, it actually consumed them. Every single Lady's Slipper pot was filled with an ugly, spongy brown mass, much to the disgust of everyone in the department.

But Bob was philosophical about this invasion of creeping goo. "I guess my information was a little off," he laughs. Fortunately, we've gotten more accurate information since this incident!

The Perennial Culture

Through Bob, I learned just what it means to be a real perennials enthusiast. A unique culture exists among perennial growers, one that sometimes makes getting the perennials he wants a challenge for Bob. There's a big difference between ordering bedding plants and ordering perennials: annuals are typically grown in huge crops by a small number of large suppliers, whereas when Bob orders perennials, he has to deal with thousands of individuals and small companies. And for many of the rare plants, there are only a few specialty growers, not all of them willing to share their favourites. It took some time for Bob to establish relationships with these growers; in a sense, he had to prove himself to each supplier, sometimes by bartering for rare plants with some special varieties he'd cajoled from still another grower. But Bob is a pretty easy guy to get along with, and he knows his stuff. Over the years, he's built up connections with perennial experts all over the world, and now he's ordering 5,000 varieties a year—quite an increase from that first 400!

Lord & Lady Strathcona with Jim Hole on a recent visit to Hole's Greenhouses & Gardens.

The Structure of Perennial Gardening

Jim and I have different but complementary outlooks on gardening. I tend to focus on the simplest, most practical means of caring for my perennials, from deciding whether or not to use snow cover to determining how often to water my clematis. Jim, on the other hand, likes to investigate the science of perennials. He's fascinated by the way different perennials have evolved to suit their climates; the sturdiness of alpine plants is just one of many examples.

Naturally, there is some overlap in our attitudes. Jim isn't obsessive about the science, and I'm not oblivious to it. Together, I think we make a pretty good team. We also get a lot of help from Bob, his chief assistant Jan Goodall, and the other knowledgeable members of our perennials staff. The field is so complex that it's almost impossible for any one person to know everything about perennials, so we stack the deck a little by hiring all the experts we can. They were also responsible for recording almost all of the questions you'll find in the following chapters.

This book is divided into seven sections that follow the progress of a typical perennial-gardening season.

The Basics

Knowing the basics can make all the difference in your garden. If there's one thing I'd recommend to perennial gardeners, it's to learn a little Latin. Common names vary widely, which can lead to confusion—what one gardener calls beebalm, another might refer to as Oswego tea, and still another as sweet bergamot. But if you know that all three are *Monarda didyma* in Latin, there's no possibility of buying the wrong plant or, even worse, giving it improper care.

Choosing Perennials

Although you should always choose the perennials that appeal to you most, it's helpful to consider the environment of your yard. When our new house was completed in the mid 1980s, I had a flowerbed right next to a wall that was heavily shaded by numerous poplars and maples. Planting several hostas filled in the bed nicely, and they continue to thrive in that cool, shady niche. Success becomes much more assured with just a little planning.

Starting, Transplanting, and Planting

Jan Goodall, another of our perennial experts, sees every season as a circle— and different plants start at different points on that circle. For a season-long display, it helps to know which plants start at what point. Different perennials need different treatments to accommodate their particular life cycles.

The Growing Season

Sometimes you learn by osmosis. "Don't fertilize perennials after August first," is a pretty standard piece of advice, and a good one: you don't want perennials to be growing actively when fall hits. When you stop fertilizing, you give the plants time to go dormant, which enables them to survive the winter. I've heard this tip repeated so often that I don't honestly remember where I learned it first. But the important thing is that I *did* learn it!

Enjoy Perennials

As I write this introduction, there are two beautiful glass vases on the counter of the perennials department's information booth, filled with an assortment of astilbe, coralbells, irises, lilies, and a few annual cutflowers thrown in for good measure. Plenty of perennials make excellent cutflowers, but there are just as many that don't—knowing which is which is essential.

Troubleshooting Perennials

Perennials usually don't cause much trouble—on the whole, they're pretty tough plants. But all plants have natural predators and inherent weaknesses, which can lead to difficulties. Jan Goodall's brother just recently started to grow perennials, and he was delighted with his delphiniums and columbine. Jan went over to see them and thought they looked lovely, too, but a few days later she received a frantic call from her brother. All of his delphiniums and columbine had been reduced to mere sticks: their foliage and flowers were gone. Jan knew exactly what had happened, since she'd had the same experience in the Hole's show garden shortly after she started working here. "You've got columbine worms," she told her brother. "All you can do now is cut those plants down to the ground and wait for next year. If they come back next season, use Latox on them—that'll take care of them."

Perennial Varieties

With the vast choices available to perennial gardeners, there's always something new to explore. If you're just trying out astilbe or can't figure out why your hosta's leaves are turning pale, here's where to turn.

The Virtue of Patience

Like an easygoing double fernleaf peony, the perennials department has grown over the years, slowly but surely. The depth and breadth of plants we carry has increased every season, and the primitive perennial manual started by Dorothy back in the beginning will soon evolve into a massive computer database. But more importantly, our collective appreciation of perennials has been enriched a hundred-fold as our exposure to their astounding diversity has increased.

CHAPTER 1 ❧
THE BASICS

The sheer variety of perennials can be a little intimidating—contrast the height and grandeur of a plume poppy with the short, stubby growth of saxifrage or the massive, light-gathering leaves of a hosta. Despite this diversity, perennials all share certain characteristics. A good grasp of the basics will ensure an enduring relationship with your perennial garden.

Definitions

What's the difference between an annual and a perennial?

Lois ❖ An annual is a plant that goes from seed to bloom and back to seed in a single season. Perennials take three years or longer to complete their life cycle.

Jim ❖ Of course, climate plays a key role in what we call an annual or a perennial. Many perennial plants from warmer climates are grown as annual bedding plants in Canada, like verbena, kniphofia, some varieties of portulaca, and ice plant.

For the purposes of this book, we'll consider a plant a perennial if its roots and crowns survive for a minimum of three growing seasons in western Canada.

What's the difference between herbaceous and woody perennials?

Jim ❖ Herbaceous perennials have soft growth above ground which dies to ground level in the winter, while woody perennials have both soft and hard growth above ground. In the winter, only the hard growth remains alive.

Strictly speaking, shrubs and trees can be considered woody perennials. However, the category also includes smaller plants ("shrublets") such as heathers and rock daphne.

Why aren't perennials just listed by their common names, instead of those funny Latin names?

Lois ❖ A single plant may have several different common names in different parts of the world. For example, the plant that I call bleeding heart is lady's locket in some places and our lady in a boat in others. However, if I use the Latin name *Dicentra spectabilis*, we know we're all talking about the same flower.

Jim ❖ Carl Linnaeus, a Swedish scientist, developed the binomial system in 1753. Under this system, every organism is classified according to its similarities to and differences from other organisms. Individual organisms are differentiated scientifically by their genus and species names. Often, the name describes specific features of a plant. For example, the genus name *Dicentra* means "two spurs," while the species name *spectabilis* means "worth seeing"—an apt description of the bleeding heart.

Brush up your Latin!

Meanings of a few common plant names

Colour

album: white; *e.g., Dictanmnus albus* (gas plant)

atropurpureum: dark purple, purplish red or purplish black; *e.g., Cimicifuga ramosa* 'Atropurpurea' (snakeroot)

aureum: golden-yellow; *e.g., Lysimachia nummularia aureum* (creeping Jenny)

caeruleum: sky-blue; *e.g., Polemonium caeruleum* (Jacob's ladder)

coccineum: scarlet; *e.g., Tanacetum coccineum* (painted daisy)

flavum: pale yellow; *e.g., Linum flavum* (yellow flax)

purpureum: purple; *e.g., Eupatorium purpureum* (Joe Pye)

roseum: pink or rose; *e.g., Alcea rosea* (hollyhock)

rubrum: red; *e.g., Filipendula rubrum* (meadowsweet)

sulphureum: sulphur-yellow; *e.g., Epimedium x sulphureum* (bishop's hat)

variegatum: variegated leaves (marked, striped or blotched with a colour other than green); *e.g., Aegopodium podagraria* 'Variegatum' (goutweed)

Dictamnus albus ❧ gas plant

Growth Habit

acaulis: stemless flowers, resting in the centre of a clump of leaves; *e.g., Gentiana acaulis* (stemless gentian)

alpinus: a plant native to the Alps or other mountainous region; usually low-growing; *e.g., Aster alpinus* (alpine aster)

cordifolia: heart-shaped leaves; often wide-leaved as well; *e.g., Bergenia cordifolia* (elephant ears)

flora-plena: double-flowered; *e.g., Saponaria officinalis flora-plena* (soapwort)

paniculata: having an open flower cluster (panicle); *e.g., Phlox paniculata* (garden phlox) or *Gypsophila paniculata* (baby's breath)

repens: creeping habit, often rooting; *e.g., Gypsophila repens* (creeping baby's breath)

spicata: spiked flowers; *e.g., Veronica spicata* (speedwell) or *Liatris spicata* (gay feather)

Potentilla sp. ❀ cinquefoil 'Gibson's Scarlet'

How long do perennials live?

Lois ❖ Some perennials, like peonies, can go on virtually forever, provided they receive regular basic care.

Jim ❖ It varies by species, but many will outlive you if you take care of them and divide them regularly.

Why do some live longer than others?

Jim ❖ Some perennials (lupines, hollyhocks) normally have a shorter life span. However, some of these will survive for years if you grow them under optimal conditions and give them regular maintenance (regular watering and fertilizing, plus division when required). Others self-seed so freely that they seem to survive for years.

Some plants are called biennials. What does that mean?

Jim ❖ A biennial normally requires two growing seasons to complete its life cycle. Most biennials grow only foliage the first year, and then flower and set seed in the second, before dying. Some examples are hollyhocks, English daisies, and forget-me-nots.

Why don't perennials bloom all summer?

Jim ❖ All living organisms share a common goal: reproduction. Blooming and producing seed, however, require a lot of energy. In addition to producing seed, perennials must also store up enough energy to survive the winter. In order to do this, most perennial species only bloom in-tensely for a short period each season.

Annual plants, because they don't need to survive the winter, can expend more energy producing blooms and setting seed. Also, plant breeders have worked extensively to develop annual varieties that bloom all season long.

Paeonia ❦ early hybrid peony 'Paula Fay'

Perennials vs. Annuals

Advantages of perennials over annuals

- Offer years of enjoyment for a one-time investment
- Provide continuity in your landscaping
- Don't need to be planted in the spring or removed in the fall
- Some emerge in early spring, before you even begin to plant annuals
- Don't require deadheading
- Offer a wide range of sizes when mature
- Provide interesting foliar textures and colors, if used properly in accents or special plantings
- Can become family heirlooms (e.g., Grandma's peony)
- Available in a very wide range of flower colours and shapes, and foliage shapes and textures

Advantages of annuals over perennials

- Cheaper per plant, on average
- Easier to eliminate weeds, because you work the entire bed every spring
- Long blooming season, with lots of flowers and colour
- Annuals are rarely invasive
- Easier to remove because they don't develop perennial root systems

Soil

What is good soil?

Lois ❖ Soil—both garden soil and potting soil—should serve your plants' needs. Good soil anchors the roots firmly, but is loose and porous enough to allow them to grow and branch extensively. It retains moisture, but has adequate drainage. It's neither too acidic nor too alkaline, and contains all the nutrients your plants require.

Why is good soil so important?

Lois ❖ Good soil is the foundation of a good garden. Grab a fistful of your soil and give it a good squeeze. Does it hold together or fall apart? If it holds together, is it still soft and springy or does it feel like a lump of clay? What colour is it?

If you have a nice, dark clump of earth that you can easily crumble between your fingers, you're well on your way. Otherwise, your first step should be to improve your soil quality.

Jim ❖ You simply can't grow a successful garden in poor soil. Creating and maintaining good loam may take some work, but no other gardening job is more important. Loam is a blend of sand, silt, clay and organic matter.

What type of soils do perennials need?

Lois ❖ Most perennials prefer well-drained, rich, balanced soil.

Jim ❖ Well-drained, rich, and balanced mean:

- Balanced—pH neither too acidic nor too alkaline (6.0–7.5)
- Well-drained—able to hold adequate moisture, while allowing any excess to drain away
- Rich—lots of organic matter, whether from compost, manure, or peat moss.

However, there are many exceptions to the rule. You must check the particular needs of every variety you plant. Cacti, for instance, prefer lots of sand and little organic matter. Ladyslippers prefer low nutrient levels.

How deep should the topsoil be?

Lois ❖ The deeper the topsoil the better, but you should start with at least 30 cm.

Jim ❖ Good, deep topsoil gives your perennials more room to establish their roots. Deep and vigorous roots are better equipped to withstand drought and to survive harsh winters.

How do I prepare a new perennial bed?

Lois ❖ First, get rid of as many weeds as possible. By starting with a clean bed, you'll save yourself countless hours of weeding in the future.

I advise people to summerfallow for one year, like farmers do. Till the soil regularly to keep the area black, making sure that weeds don't get a chance to grow or produce seed.

Jim ❖ If you're starting from scratch, I recommend at least 30 cm of good topsoil, with lots of organic matter.

If you're using an area that has already been cultivated, it's essential to eliminate perennial weeds and other undesirable plants. Allow plants to grow in spring to a height of 15 cm, then spray the area with Roundup. It may take several applications to get rid of problem weeds like thistle and quackgrass.

Why is good drainage important?

Lois ❖ Waterlogged soil severely injures most perennials. Proper drainage is a good idea for any perennial, but it's critical for plants like bitterroot and bearded iris.

Jim ❖ Roots grow poorly in waterlogged soil. In fact, they may eventually die due to lack of oxygen. Waterlogged soil also leaves the plant vulnerable to disease. To make matters worse, many beneficial soil microorganisms die in waterlogged soil.

Waterlogged soils can freeze in early winter, damaging the roots and crown. In the spring, water must be able to drain away, so that the crowns don't remain constantly wet.

How do I check to see if my soil has proper drainage?

Jim ❖ Dig a hole 20-30 cm deep, fill it with water, and watch. The water should drain away slowly but steadily, leaving the hole empty within an hour. If the water just sits, the drainage is poor. Work in plenty of organic matter to improve the drainage.

If, on the other hand, the water drains out of the hole almost immediately, you have too much drainage. This won't necessarily harm your plants, but it does mean you'll have to water more frequently.

Soil Tests

What is a soil test, and when should I get one?

Lois ❖ A soil test measures the various components that make up your soil and determines if it is pH balanced. You should get your soil tested if you have a very large garden or acreage, or if you have a history of plants growing poorly in a specific area despite proper care.

Jim ❖ If you have specific problem areas in your garden, it's a good idea to do a soil test. You can learn as much from a soil test as you would from several years of trial and error.

What does a soil test tell me?

Jim ❖ A basic soil test tells you:

- Levels of the major nutrients—nitrogen (N), phosphorus (P), and potassium (K) (these are the 3 numbers on a fertilizer label; thus, 10-52-10 is 10N-52P-10K). Sulphur levels are also sometimes included.
- pH level—the soil's acidity or alkalinity.
- Soluble salts—plants burn if the concentration is too high.
- Soil texture—the relative quantities of sand, silt, clay, and organic matter.
- An advanced soil test also includes the levels of the minor nutrients: iron (Fe), molybdenum (Mo), sulphur (S), magnesium (Mg), and calcium (Ca).

For farmers, it can be very expensive not to test soil. For example, a deficiency of 20 kg of nitrogen per hectare adds up to a 10,000-kg shortage on a 500-hectare farm. That shortfall could result in catastrophic crop-yield losses.

Thankfully, the stakes aren't quite as high for home gardeners. However, if you're having trouble growing healthy plants, it's worth spending a few dollars to test and improve your soil.

Should I get test the pH in my garden?

Lois ❖ Yes. Test your soil pH once every couple of years

Jim ❖ Soil pH strongly influences how well your perennials absorb nutrients, and also affects the health of the soil microbial population. In short, a pH that's too high or too low leads to an unhealthy garden.

It's imperative that you take a good representative sample. To do this, take a small trowel and dig down 30 cm into the soil and place the sample in a bucket. Take half a dozen samples like this from the area of your garden that you want to test.

Why is my soil's pH important?

Jim ❖ First, let's review our chemistry. pH is a scale for measuring acidity or alkalinity. On this scale, 7.0 is neutral—neither acidic nor alkaline. As the numbers decrease (6.9, 6.8 etc.), the acidity increases. As the numbers rise (7.1, 7.2 etc.), the alkalinity increases.

In alkaline soil, many essential nutrients remain bound up as insoluble compounds. This means that your plants have a harder time absorbing them from the soil.

Most perennials perform best in slightly acidic soil (6.2-6.5). However, when the pH is too low, the plants tend to absorb excessive quantities of nutrients, particularly metals like iron and zinc, which can be toxic. As well, many beneficial soil microorganisms cannot survive in very acidic soils.

How do I adjust my soil's pH?

Lois ❖ Assuming you have tested your soil's pH, take the results to a good garden centre. A staff member should be able to give you reliable advice on how to deal with your soil's pH.

Jim ❖ To adjust the pH, you must amend your soil. Sulphur lowers your soil's pH (making it more acidic) while horticultural lime raises the pH (making it more alkaline). You can purchase these products at most garden centres.

If you're adding sulphur, stick with very fine sulphur or aluminum sulphate—coarse sulphur reacts too slowly. Use dolomitic lime, because it contains both calcium and magnesium (two important plant nutrients). Be sure to buy a fine grade; otherwise the lime will react too slowly in the soil.

How much sulphur/lime to add to soil to change pH levels

GARDEN SULPHUR* 0.5 kg/100 m² (acidifier—to lower pH)

Desired pH Change	Sands	Loam	Clay
8.5–6.5	46	57	68
8.0–6.5	27	34	46
7.5–6.5	11	18	23
7.0–6.5	2	3	6

* although sulphur is effective, it is slow to react to soil

LIMESTONE 0.5 kg/100 m² (basifier—to increase pH)

Desired pH Change	Sandy loam	Loam	Silt Loam	Clay
4.0–6.5	115	160	193	230
4.5–6.5	96	133	193	230
5.0–6.5	78	105	128	151
5.5–6.5	60	78	91	105
6.0–6.5	32	41	50	55

I have limestone rocks in my rock garden. Will they adversely affect the soil pH?

Jim ❖ No. Large rocks don't break down very quickly! As a result, they don't significantly affect the chemistry of the surrounding soil.

In any case, most rock-garden perennials actually prefer slightly alkaline conditions. Their natural habitat usually consists of calcareous (limey) soil.

Some perennials for alkaline soil

baby's breath
blue sage
campion
elephant ears
goldenrod
hens & chicks
hops
lady's mantle
lamium
lupine
plume poppy
poppy
potentilla
sage
saxifrage
soapwort
statice
stonecrop
yarrow
yucca

Adding to the Soil

Can I improve the quality of my soil or is it best to remove it and bring in new soil?

Lois ❖ Unless your soil is absolutely dreadful, there's no reason to start entirely from scratch. Add peat moss, well-rotted manure, and compost to help your soil out.

Jim ❖ If you do have extremely poor soil, invest in a load of good topsoil. You'll save yourself an awful lot of hard work and frustration.

Buy your soil only from a reputable dealer. Look for soil rich in organic matter, with a nice, fairly loose texture.

Should I add anything to the soil in an established perennial bed?

Lois ❖ Even if you're blessed with good soil, you still have to work to maintain it. Add organic matter every fall and spring, if possible.

Jim ❖ Rich topsoil is best and easiest, but well-rotted manure, compost, leaf mould, peat moss, and commercial fertilizers also help to improve your perennial bed.

Each fall, dig up the soil around your perennials and add organic matter.

Does adding perlite to clay-like garden soil help it drain better? Is it the best solution for poor drainage?

Lois ❖ It's one solution, but it's not the best or cheapest alternative. You'd be better off adding peat moss, manure, and compost.

Jim ❖ Perlite does help clay soil to drain better. However, perlite particles aren't very strong and can break down very quickly, especially if you work the soil with a rototiller. The other problem with perlite is that you need a tremendous amount to improve drainage, which is very expensive. It also blows away very easily in light winds. Instead, I recommend using plenty of organic matter. It's far cheaper, lasts much longer, and improves the soil texture.

I think that my soil is deficient in iron. What should I do?

Jim ❖ If you're really worried, you might consider investing in a soil test. However, if you believe your plants aren't absorbing enough iron, the problem might just be the pH of your soil. If your soil is too alkaline, the iron won't be available for your plants.

Iron in alkaline soil is like sugar in an ice-cold glass of water—it's not very soluble. Lowering the soil's pH is like warming up that glass of water: the lower the pH, the more easily iron is absorbed.

If your soil has a high pH, lower it with aluminum sulphate or very fine sulphur. You can also add chelated iron to the soil—in alkaline soil, chelated iron works much better than regular iron.

Campanula persicifolia ❧
peachleaf bellflower

What should I do about evergreen needles in my flowerbeds? Is there any way to neutralize the acidity from the needles?

Lois ❖ Lime counteracts the acidity of the needles. It would take an awful lot of evergreen needles, however, to significantly lower a soil's pH. Test your soil before assuming that acidity is the problem.

Jim ❖ Use dolomitic lime, because it contains both calcium and magnesium (two important plant nutrients). Be sure to buy a fine grade; otherwise the lime will react too slowly in the soil.

However, if you've got a flowerbed that's doing poorly beneath an evergreen tree, don't necessarily blame the needles! Acidity is often not the problem. Evergreens are shady, and their roots absorb a great deal of water. Even if the pH is perfectly balanced, you'll have a hard time growing plants under or near your tree.

Convallaria majalis ❧ lily-of-the-valley

Do any perennials grow under pine or spruce trees?

Jim ❖ Few perennials can tolerate dry, shady conditions, like you'd find under pine trees. Try using bergenia or barrenwort as a groundcover.

My neighbour heard that adding sulphur to the garden will help her plants. What effect does sulphur have?

Lois ❖ Your neighbour is right—if the soil is too alkaline. Adding sulphur makes the soil more acidic, which is great for the many plants that prefer neutral soil.

Jim ❖ You can add sulphur for two different reasons: to lower the soil pH or to increase the amount of sulphur in sulphur-deficient soils. The sulphur you add must be very fine (microfine or superfine) in order to react quickly with your soil. It can take months for coarse sulphur to break down in your soil. Use aluminum sulphate or iron sulphate, which react quickly with the soil.

Hosta ❦ hosta 'Christmas Tree'

Should I add lime to my soil?

Lois ❖ Lime doesn't solve all gardening problems, but it is good for neutralizing acid soils. If you're adding the lime directly into your garden, do it in the fall after everything's cleaned up, or first thing in the spring.

Jim ❖ Lime adjusts the pH of a soil by neutralizing the acidity of components like peat moss. There's no reason to add lime, however, unless your soil is very acidic. Also, bear in mind that some perennials prefer acidic soil.

Some perennials for acidic soil

anemone
astilbe
beardtongue
bishop's hat
blue himalayan poppy
daylily
elephant ears
gentian
goatsbeard
goutweed
hosta
lily-of-the-valley
meadow rue
meadowsweet
moor grass
ostrich fern
primrose
pulmonaria
shooting-star
snakeroot
Solomon's seal

Filipendula rubra 'Venusta' ❧ meadowsweet

CHAPTER 2 ❦
CHOOSING PERENNIALS

Choosing the right perennials for your garden is, above all, a matter of taste— delphiniums were my favourite when I was a young girl growing up in Saskatchewan. But there are other things to keep in mind when shopping for perennials, too. How much room do you have? Do you want to attract hummingbirds or butterflies? Are you up to the challenge of trying a few out-of-zone plants in your northern garden? Choosing the right perennial to suit your needs is part science and part art. Here are the most popular questions we've had on the subject.

What main factors should I consider when choosing varieties?

Lois ❖ I could spend the rest of the book answering this question! There are so many factors to consider, but the most important points are how much room you have, how much sunlight your garden receives, and what your soil is like. Past that, it's largely a matter of personal taste!

When you make your trip to the garden centre, ask the staff for their recommendations. Arm yourself with a good reference book, and allow yourself plenty of time to shop around.

Jim ❖ You'll also want to think seriously about how much work you're willing to devote to your garden. If a particular variety requires a bit of extra maintenance, by all means buy it, but only if you can take care of it properly.

Finally, your budget also obviously comes into play. You may have to adjust your choices based on the money you have to spend.

I want to plant a small garden that needs no care, and perennials seem like the perfect solution. What should I plant?

Lois ❖ There is simply no such thing as a care-free garden! Every garden requires basic care, especially regular watering and weeding. However, some perennials can get by with very little maintenance—including grasses, cactus and alpines.

Should I mix my annuals and perennials together, or keep them in separate areas of my garden?

Lois ❖ Go ahead and mix them, by all means! Because perennials have shorter blooming periods, and bloom at different times of year, it's nice to have the annuals in there to provide an ongoing burst of colour.

Jim ❖ By mixing together annuals and perennials, you multiply the number of available combinations. If plants complement each other's textures, colours, and growth habits, then plant them together.

Zones

What's a zone?

Lois ❖ Zones are regions that have similar winter temperatures. The higher the zone number (from 0 to 10), the milder the winter. Perennials are often rated for their hardiness, using these zone numbers. For instance, a plant rated hardy to zone 5 is at risk for winter injury in a zone 4 garden.

Jim ❖ In Canada, climate zones are ranked from 0 to 9, based on an area's coldest winter temperatures. Northern ranges of Alberta, Saskatchewan, and Manitoba all have ranges considered zone 0. Some regions in the Vancouver and Victoria areas are rated 9a, meaning that they have the mildest winters in the country.

Snow cover and mulches can significantly increase a plant's chance of surviving a harsh winter. For example, it's not uncommon for zone 5 plants to survive in a zone 3 region that receives lots of snow.

In other words, use these numbers only as guidelines—in the end, there's no way to tell whether a plant will survive unless you give it a try!

How do I know what the zone is where I live?

Lois ❖ Simply find your community on a climate zones map.

Jim ❖ The map gives the official answer. However, in practice, you often find several different climatic conditions in a single region, or even in a single yard! For instance, a tender perennial that would die out in a zone 3 garden might overwinter just fine if you plant it next to your house's foundation in a sheltered area.

I live in a zone 4 area, but want to try some more tender perennials. Can I try perennials rated to zone 5? Zone 6?

Lois ❖ I live in zone 3a, and have seen plenty of zone 5 and zone 6 perennials survive the winter. The bigger the gap between a plant's rating and your climatic zone number, the more winter protection it requires. You also have to be philosophical when you lose the occasional plant!

Jim ❖ Your odds will be better if you live in an area that gets a lot of snow. Under a good, thick, insulating blanket of snow, many relatively tender perennials will survive even when outside temperatures drop very low.

Some perennials for shady spots

anemone
astilbe
bishop's hat
bleeding heart
blue Himalayan poppy
coralbell
creeping jenny
elephant ears
gentian
globeflower
goatsbeard
goutweed
honeysuckle
hosta
lady's mantle
lamium
lily-of-the-valley
masterwort
meadowsweet
monkshood
ostrich fern
primrose
pulmonaria
rayflower
shooting-star
snakeroot
Solomon's seal

Why do local stores sell perennials that are not hardy in my area?

Jim ❖ Hardiness seems like a simple concept initially—the colder the winter, the greater the likelihood that your perennials will die. However, this is a gross oversimplification.

We have good friends in Chicago who are professional growers. You may assume that, with their warmer winters, they could easily grow anything we can. However, their warmer winter actually poses problems for some perennials. For instance, rain often saturates the soil, causing roots to rot or plant crowns to freeze in blocks of ice. Their warmer summer weather can also be detrimental. Heat stress and and humidity devastates many perennials.

For most perennials, deep and persistent snow cover is ideal—that's why in our area we successfully grow many perennials that are not thought of as "hardy."

Locations

What is shade? Sun?

Jim ❖ Shade and sun are very difficult to define precisely. Let's take shade, for example. There's light shade, dappled shade, morning shade, and deep shade—none of which are quantifiable.

For simplicity, I define a shade location as one that receives no direct sunlight all day long. Partial shade means morning sun until 11:00 am and then dappled sunlight until the early evening. A full-sun location receives six hours or more of unobstructed sunlight.

Shopping for Perennials

Shopping by Mail

Usually when I order perennials by mail they come as roots, but once the plant I ordered came in a pot and was already growing. Which is better?

Lois ❖ Many people are surprised when plants arrive in pots and are already growing actively. This results in a quicker start, and a better and bigger plant, earlier. I always prefer to ship (and receive) plants this way.

Jim ❖ The main difficulty with shipping dormant plants is that it is impossible to tell if the plants are alive.

A few times when I have ordered perennials by mail, the companies have asked if I want substitutions. Why can't I get the plants I ordered?

Lois ❖ Plants are living things, and mailorder companies can't just order up more if they run out. For some plants (some perennials and especially trees and shrubs) it can take 2 to 5 years or longer before the plants are large enough to be sold.

Jim ❖ Other reasons for shortages could be that pests have destroyed a crop. Demand can simply exceed supply. Weather can also play a factor: cool, cloudy weather can delay plant growth so that plants are too small and not shippable when the order is being processed.

How far away can I order plants from?

Lois ❖ You can obtain plants from around the world, but often you can only order from within your own country. People are always surprised that we ship right across Canada. Shipping plants by express gives them 1-3 days in transit. Plants will do fine for a few days in a box if they are packed and shipped properly.

Jim ❖ If you order plants from outside Canada, they must be shipped bare root and have a phyto-sanitary certificate. This costs more and also means there will be restriction on the kinds of plants customs will allow across the border.

What should I do when my plants arrive?

Lois ❖ When you receive your order, **unpack it right away** (remember to pick up your order from the post office right away). Water the plants if they need it and place them in a shaded or morning-sun location.

Jim ❖ Do not, as one poor woman did, water your wilted plants and place them in full sun all day! Check your plants for to see if they need water every day.

Do not leave plants inside the home or garage. If it is above freezing, put them outdoors during the day at least and bring them in at night if necessary.

Your plants will do far better if they are planted as soon as possible (unless temperatures are still below freezing). It is much more stressful for the plants to sit in pots for days on end.

When I'm shopping, how do I recognize which plants are healthiest?

Lois ❖ Don't buy a plant that's spindly, wilted, or damaged in any way; it will almost certainly disappoint you in the long run.

Jim ❖ Look for stocky, well-branched specimens with healthy leaves.

I notice that a large perennial in a big pot costs quite a lot more than a smaller plant of the exact same variety. Should I spend the extra money?

Lois ❖ It depends on your budget and your level of patience. A big plant provides instant results, whereas a small one might take a couple of years to fully come into its own. On the other hand, you could take that money and buy several small plants of different varieties—provided you're willing to wait a couple of years for them to mature.

Jim ❖ Mom's right—those small plants look like they are a great buy, but only if you're patient enough to wait for them to grow.

Perennials don't mature overnight. Those big plants took several years to mature, which is why they're often more expensive. If you buy a large plant, it will it look better initially and you'll also be able to divide it that much sooner.

Our perennials staff members were abuzz last summer when a customer loaded several shopping carts with the largest, lushest plants he could find. It seems he had volunteered to display his garden as part of a rather prestigious garden tour. He wanted to fill in a few gaps here and there—and fill them in quickly!

Why are some perennials so expensive?

Lois ❖ Plant breeding can be a long, difficult, and very expensive process. A plant breeder might spend years developing a particular variety, so it's not surprising the resulting plants cost more.

One day in our perennials area, I chatted with a couple from Calgary. The wife told me that she was here to pick up her anniversary present. Her husband explained, "I asked her what she wanted, and she told me 'a yellow peony.' I didn't think that was much to ask for, until she told me how much it cost—$90."

Jim ❖ Sounds like she was a real collector. Yellow peonies are very rare and grow slowly. They take years to germinate, and three to five more years to flower.

Believe it or not, though, $90 is cheap compared to the prices of the world's rarest perennials. For instance, there's a single hybrid hosta in Japan valued at $10,000, and you can easily spend over $4000 on rare hepaticas.

Some unusual perennials to try

pheasant's eye (*Adonis*)
ginger (*Asarum*)
wax bells (*Kirengeshoma*)
lenten rose (*Helleborus*)
species peonies
gentian (*Gentiana*)

Hemerocallis ❦ daylily 'Terminator'

Which perennials are the most fragrant?

Lois ❖ Many perennials have wonderfully fragrant flowers or foliage. The following chart lists some of my personal favourites.

Don't hide these away at the back of your flowerbeds—put them near your deck, close to open windows, or along pathways. That way, you'll be able to enjoy them every time you pass by.

Some perennials for fragrance

beebalm (foliage)
daylily (some varieties)
gasplant (flowers, foliage)
lily-of-the-valley (flowers)
peony (flowers)
phlox (garden phlox)
pink (flower)
primrose (auricula types)
Russian sage (foliage)
sage (foliage)
soapwort (flower)
thyme (foliage)

Some perennials that attract hummingbirds

beardtongue
(*Penstemon* spp.)
beebalm (*Monarda didyma*)
bleeding hearts (*Dicentra*)
butterfly weed
(*Asclepias tuberosa*)
columbine (*Aguilegia* spp.)
coral bells
(*Heuchera sanguinea*)
daylily (*Hemerocallis*)
foxglove (*Digitalis*)
hollyhock (*Alcea rosea*)
pinks (*Dianthus*)

Some perennials that attract butterflies

aster (*Aster* spp.)
black-eyed susan
(*Rudbeckia* spp.)
coneflower
(*Echinacea* spp.)
false sunflower (*Heliopsis*)
globe thistle (*Echinops* sp.)
goldenrod (*Solidago* spp.)
Joe Pye
(*Eupatorium* spp.)
ornamental onion
(*Allium* spp.)
rockcress (*Arabis* sp.)
sneezeweed
(*Helenium* spp.)
St. John's wort
(*Hypericum* sp.)
tickseed (*Coreopsis* spp.)

Which perennials attract hummingbirds and butterflies?

Lois ❖ I've never met anyone who doesn't love hummingbirds! If you plant the flowers they prefer, chances are you'll be able to glimpse them from time to time.

Jim ❖ Hovering requires a lot more energy than flying, so hummingbirds need to eat four to six times every hour. If you offer them a reliable source of food, they can be extremely faithful visitors. One or two well-placed feeders will also help make your garden a popular stop for these very small, very hungry birds.

Bird-pollinated plants share a number of common features. They produce lots of thin nectar, often in trumpet-shaped flowers. They're not particularly fragrant, because birds lack a keen sense of smell. Red and yellow blooms are the most common shades, along with other vibrant colours such as purples, oranges, and blues.

How do I attract butterflies to my perennial garden?

Lois ❖ Like hummingbirds, butterflies require nectar. The plants in the following list attract butterflies as well as hummingbirds.

Jim ❖ Butterflies are cold-blooded and have a hard time flying in cool weather. That's why you often spot them basking in the sun, but rarely see any on brisk, cloudy days.

If you plant your perennials in a sheltered, sunny spot, the butterflies will spend much more time in your garden.

Are any perennials poisonous?

Lois ❖ Several perennials are poisonous, but I've never worried about toxicity when choosing plants. It's extremely unlikely that a passing animal or child would eat enough plant material to suffer injury.

Jim ❖ A few perennials deserve a bit of extra caution, such as lily-of-the-valley, ornamental rhubarb, and monkshood. Remember, though, that toxicity is always directly related to dosage. Most poisonous plants are extremely bitter—any adult, child, or pet would be unlikely to keep eating after the first tiny nibble.

Why do some of the plant tags give different height/bloom information than the signs in my garden centre?

Jim ❖ Climate plays a large role in height and bloom time. Tag manufacturers usually base their estimates on the average temperatures for North America. In warmer climates, perennials tend to emerge earlier, bloom earlier and grow taller than they do in cooler climates.

At your garden centre, the signs (and the staff) should be able to predict more reliably how specific plants perform in your local climate.

What are groundcover perennials?

Lois ❖ As the name suggests, groundcover perennials cover the ground, like a thick, living carpet. They often thrive where few other plants will grow, such as on steep slopes and under trees. They reduce water loss, prevent soil erosion, crowd out most weeds, and require very little maintenance.

Some groundcover perennials

anemone
clematis (species types)
cranesbill
creeping jenny
  (sun or shade)
elephant ears
  (sun or shade)
fleeceflower
goutweed (sun or shade)
hops
lady's mantle
lamium
lily-of-the-valley
potentilla
sage
snow-in-summer
Solomon's seal
stonecrop
thyme

Some perennials for rock gardens

anemone
aster (alpine types)
baby's breath
   (creeping types)
beardtongue
bellflower (some)
bishop's hat
bitterroot
bleeding Heart
   (fernleaf types)
blue fescue
blue oat grass
candytuft
catmint
coralbell
cranesbill
creeping jenny
elephant ears
flax
gentian
hens & chicks
hosta (dwarf types)
moor grass
ornamental onion
   (Turkestan)
pasqueflower
phlox (creeping types)
pink
poppy (Iceland)
potentilla
primrose
rockcress
sage (some types)
saxifrage
sea thrift
shooting-star
spurge
stonecrop
strawberry
thyme
tickseed

What groundcover would you use instead of grass?

Lois ❖ Any of the thymes would be a good choice—they're low–growing, fast-spreading, and quite sturdy. Remember, though, that you can't constantly walk on groundcovers like you would grass.

Jim ❖ Grass is your best choice for durability, because its growing point is below the soil. Even if you chop the plant down to soil level, it continues to grow. Groundcovers like thyme have their growing points above the soil. They can't withstand being continually crushed or mown.

I am trying to create a woodland garden. What plants might be suitable? And what do I need to do to the soil?

Jim ❖ The following chart lists some of the best plants for woodland gardens. Because these plants are adapted to growing in woodlands, the soil in your bed should reflect that. Woodland plants love leafy, organic soil, so mix in plenty of peat moss, leaf mould, and compost.

Geranium cinereum ❦ greyleaf cranesbill 'Ballerina'

How do I create a natural-looking alpine garden?

Jim ❖ Here are a few basic tips.

- Build your rock garden in the fall and wait until the following spring before adding plants. This gives the soil a chance to settle.
- As with any new flowerbed, do your utmost to eliminate all perennial weeds before planting.
- Build up a slope, to better display your low-growing plants.
- In the spring, top up the soil in the areas that have settled.
- Gather together your plants and rocks. Spend some time moving them around until you find an arrangement you like.
- Put the rocks in their final positions, and plant your perennials.

Some woodland perennials

anemone
astilbe
bishop's hat
bleeding heart
gentian
goatsbeard
Jacob's ladder
lily (martagon types)
lily-of-the-valley
masterwort
meadowsweet
ostrich fern
primrose
shooting-star
snakeroot
Solomon's seal

What is the difference between alpine plants and rock-garden plants?

Jim ❖ Alpine plants are a subcategory of rock-garden plants. Any small plant suitable for a rock garden can be called a "rock-garden plant."

Unlike other rock-garden plants, though, alpine plants grow above the treeline in mountains. They tend to be compact, low-growing, and very hardy, which makes them ideal for rock gardens.

When buying perennials, is it better to pick a small plant or a more mature one that is already quite tall?

Lois ❖ If you want an instant garden, always pick large plants. If you don't mind waiting, though, smaller plants are less expensive.

Jim ❖ Many perennials must be at a certain level of maturity before they'll bloom. Larger plants are usually capable of blooming the first year. Large, vigorous plants adapt to the garden more quickly and fill a spot faster.

How do I choose my perennials so I have a succession of blooms all year?

Lois ❖ Most perennials have relatively short blooming periods. You can still create a steady show of colour in your perennial bed, however, if you choose an assortment of perennials that bloom at different times of the year.

In each bed, plant some perennials that bloom in the spring, some that bloom in the summer, and some that bloom in the fall. You can also group them according to colour—creating a blue bed, a red bed, a pink bed, etc.

What perennials are really true blue?

Lois ❖ A lot of flowers out there are called blue, even though they are closer to purple. That's why we call the plants with truly blue petals "true blue." In our books, this includes the blue Himalayan poppy, gentians, speedwell, iris and bellflower.

Gentiana sp. ❧ gentian

Primula vialii ❧ Litton's primrose

Which perennials are...

...fall-blooming?
asters
Helen's flower (*Helenium*)
mums (*Dendranthemum*)
obedient plant (*Physostegia*)\
Scotch heather (*Calluna vulgaris*)
stonecrop (*Sedum*)

...for in and around ponds?
cardinal flower (*Lobelia cardinalis*)
creeping jenny (*Lysimachia nummularia*)
Japanese iris (*Iris ensata*)
marsh marigold (*Caltha palustris*)
rayflower (*Ligularia* spp.)
spiral rush (*Juncus effusus spiralis*)

...showy and shade-tolerant?
alumroot (*Heuchera*)
astilbe
bleeding Heart (*Dicentra*)
fumitory (*Corydalis*)
globeflower (*Trollius*)
hostas
Joe Pye weed (*Eupatorium*)
martagon lilies (*Lilium martagon*)
meadowsweet (*Filipendula*)
monkshood (*Aconitum*)
mossy maxifrages (*Saxifraga arendsii*)
primroses (*Primula* spp.)

...for an English cottage garden?
baby's breath (*Gypsophila*)
columbine (*Aquilegia*)
daylily (*Hemerocallis*)
delphiniums
erigeron
false sunflower (*Heliopsis*)
garden phlox
globe thistle (*Echinops*)
iris
lilies
meadow rue (*Thalictrum*)

monkshood (*Aconitum*)
painted daisy (*Tanacetum*)
peonies
Shasta daisy (*Leucanthemum*)

...herbs?
beebalm (*Monarda didyma*)
evening primrose
foxglove (*Digitalis*)
St. John's Wort (*Hypericum*)
wormwood (*Artemisia*)
thymes

...first to bloom in the spring?
adonis
alpine snowbells (*soldanella*)
candytuft (*iberis*)
draba
liverleaf (*Hepatica*)
marsh marigold (*Caltha*)
Pulsatilla
rock jasmine (*Androsace*)
saxifrage
stonecress (*Eunomia*)

...white?
aster
baby's breath (*Gypsophila*)
bearded and Siberian iris
bellflower (*Campanula*)
bleeding heart (*Dicentra*)
candytuft (*Iberis*)
clematis
cornflower (*Centaurea*)
delphiniums
flax (*Linum*)
garden mum (*Leucanthemum*)
garden phlox
lilies (*Lilium*)
peonies (*Paeonia*)
rockcress (*Arabis*)
Shasta daisy (*Leucanthemum*)

...for growing under trees?
bergenia
bishop's hat (*Epimedium*)
creeping stonecrop (*Sedum*)
Himalayan fleeceflower (*Persicaria*)
lily-of-the-valley (*Convallaria*)
snow-in-summer (*Cerastium*)
white archangel (*Lamium*)

...showy groundcovers?
bugle flower (*Ajuga*)
fleeceflower (*Persicaria*)
thyme (*Thymus* spp.)
white archangel (*Lamium*)

...fast-growing groundcovers?
creeping jenny (*Lysimachia*)
snow on the mountain (*Aegopodium*)
white archangel (*Lamium*)
woolly mother of thyme
  (*Thymus pseudolanuginosus*)

...groundcovers for garden paths?
Erigeron leionurus
hypsela
Irish/Scotch moss (*Sagina*)
moss campion (*Silene acaulis*)
thyme

...spike-flowered?
delphinium
foxglove
foxtail lily
liatris
rayflower
obedient plant
speedwell
yucca

Phlox paniculata ❧ garden phlox 'Eva Cullum'

What are some perennials with interesting foliage?

Lois ❖ Foliage is an important consideration with perennials, since few perennials bloom for more than a short period each year. The following perennials look beautiful throughout the growing season, and some of them produce lovely flowers as well.

bishop's hat (*Epimedium*)
blue fescue (*Festuca*)
coralbell (Alumroot)
daylily (*Hemetocallis*)
elephant ear (*Bergenia*)
ferns
flax (*Linium*)
goutweed (*Aegopodium*)
hens & chicks (*Sempervivum*)
hops (*Humulus lupulus*)
hosta
iris
lady's mantle (*Alchemilla*)
lamb's ears (*Stachys byzantina*)
lungwort (*Pulmonaria*)

lupine
moor grass (*Molima*)
ornamental rhubarb (*Rheum*)
ostrich fern (*Matteucia*)
plume poppy (*Macleaya*)
rayflower (*Ligularia*)
Russian sage (*Perovskia*)
sage (*Artemisia*)
saxifrage
sea holly (*Eryngium*)
snakeroot (*Cimicifuga*)
snow-in-summer
stonecrop (*Sedum*)
thyme (*Thymus*)
white archangel (*Lamium*)
yucca

Stachys byzantina ❧ lamb's ears

CHAPTER 3 ✺
STARTING, TRANSPLANTING
& PLANTING

Even for perennials experts, knowing when and how to begin is often a process of trial and error. My troubles with the blue Himalayan poppy are a prime example: after trying everything I knew to get them to germinate, I gave up and threw the flats in a corner on a cool cement floor. The cool floor was just what the seeds needed, and they sprang up like mad. Sometimes you get lucky, but I wish I'd known about the seeds' need for a cold treatment before I'd gone through all of that struggling!

Direct Seeding Perennials

Some perennials to direct seed

alpine pink
(Dianthus alpinus)
bellflower (Campanula)
black-eyed susan
(Rudbeckia)
blue flax (Linum)
common harebill
(Campanula)
columbine (Aquilegia)
delphinium
dwarf lance coreopsis
evening primrose
(Oenothera)
forget-me-not (Myosotis)
foxglove (Digitalis)
gasplant (Dictamnus)
hollyhock (Alcea)
Jacob's ladder
(Polemonium)
lilies
lupine
Maltese cross (Lychnis)
mountain phlox
plains coreopsis
poppy (Papever)
primrose (Primula)
purple coneflower
(Echinacea)
Shasta daisy
(Leucanthemum)
sweet william (biennial)
sweet rocket (biennial)
thyme
violas
yarrow (Achillea)

Can I sow perennial seeds directly into my garden? Which ones?

Lois ❖ You can sow some perennials, provided you start with fresh, high-quality seed. Sow your seeds in the early spring—unless your plants have a full season to produce foliage and roots, they likely won't survive the winter. Seed more thickly than usual because, as a rule, perennial seeds have a much lower germination rate than annuals.

Jim ❖ You have to exercise patience, because perennials started from seed may take a year or two to mature. Most of them won't flower until at least their second year. If you don't want to wait that long, buy your plants from a greenhouse.

Should I sow seeds in the spring or fall?

Jim ❖ It depends on the variety. If you check the seed packet, you should be able to find reliable recommendations.

If you're unsure of the best time to sow, seed directly into the garden in late fall. Next spring, you can move the seedlings to their desired locations once they're big enough to transplant.

Starting Seeds Indoors

What do I need to start perennials indoors?

Jim ❖ If you've ever started annuals indoors, you may already have everything you need. In addition to your seeds, you'll need seedling trays, grow lights (or a bright, sunny window), seedling mix, vermiculite, fertilizer, pest-control products, and a good misting bottle.

Why do I have trouble starting my perennial seeds indoors?

Jim ❖ Perennial seeds vary tremendously in what they require in order to germinate and can be a real challenge.

They may need to be frozen and thawed (a process called stratification), etching by acid baths, or physical scraping (scarification). Some refuse to germinate if they're exposed to light, some won't germinate without it. Some need warmth, others like it cool.

Stratification and scarification break the seeds' natural dormancy. Many perennial seeds are protected by tough seed coats, which don't allow moisture to penetrate. Before the seeds can germinate, these coats must be weakened or broken—either naturally or artificially. The reason behind this is simple. If a seed fell to the ground in October and immediately germinated, the new seedling would be killed off by the first hard frost. Instead, the seed remains dormant throughout the winter. During the freezing and thawing cycles of winter and spring, the seed coat gradually breaks down. When the weather begins to warm up in the spring, the seed absorbs moisture and germinates—right at the beginning of the growing season.

How to start perennials indoors

1. Fill a seedling flat to within 1/2 inch (1 cm) of the top with a good-quality seedling mixture (a potting soil with a high percentage of peat moss and perlite). Never use garden soil as it may contain insects and disease organisms that cause root rot.
2. As a general rule, plant seeds no deeper than the thickness of the seed.
3. Water just enough to moisten the soil. Use a misting bottle with a fine spray so you don't wash away the seeds as you water.
4. Never allow the seedling mix to become dry. Germinating seeds will not tolerate dry soil and often die if the soil dries out for even a short time.
5. To get the best possible germination, use a fungacide shortly after planting to prevent 'damping off' (rotting of seedlings).
6. Cover the seedling flat with a plastic wrap or a plastic dome to increase humidity. Make a few slits in the plastic wrap to allow ventilation and prevent overheating. Remove the plastic covering once seedlings have fully emerged.
7. Tag each container with the date planted and the variety of seed.
8. Use grow lights to enhance germination and growth.
9. When seedlings produce their second set of leaves, fertilize with a 'plant starter' fertilizer, such as 10-52-10, at one quarter strength, once a week. If your seedlings are crowded, transplant them into larger containers.

Plants vary greatly in their seedling-to-maturity intervals. Most perennials should be started in February or early March. Transplant them into the garden once the risk of spring frost has passed.

Which perennials are easiest to start from seed?

Lois ❖ Choose seeds that don't require any special treatment, germinate within a month, and grow quickly once they germinate.

Jim ❖ Read the seed packets carefully. They'll give you a good idea whether or not you should try starting the seeds yourself.

Can I collect and save seed from my perennials?

Lois ❖ Propagating perennials from seed can be a long and frustrating experience. In most cases you're better off starting with plants from a garden centre or seeds from a packet.

Jim ❖ Again, it depends on the variety. Some perennials are best propagated by cuttings or division. And if a plant is a hybrid, many of the resulting offspring will not be identical to the parent.

If you are interested in saving seed, however, some of the best candidates include columbine *(Aquilegia)*, peony, delphinium, shooting star *(Dodecatheon)*, European pasque flower *(Pulsatilla vulgaris),* and yucca.

How do I know when to pick the seed?

Lois ❖ You must wait until the seed matures; otherwise, it won't germinate. Check the seeds regularly, and gather them once the colour deepens and they're no longer soft. If you wait too long, however, the seed capsules (pods, etc.) will "shatter," or break open, dispersing the seeds.

Campanula cochlearifolia ❧ spiral bellflower

Some perennials easily started from seed

bellflower
blanketflower
campion
candytuft
catmint
flax
foxglove
hollyhock
Jacob's ladder
poppy (Iceland)
potentilla
Shasta daisy
snow-in-summer
soapwort
thyme
yarrow

Birth of a Hybrid

Let's say, for instance, that you are a plant breeder, and you want to combine the intense red flower colour of one variety with the disease resistance of another. First, you must select and isolate two parent lines: one with the intense colour and the other with the disease resistance.

You inbreed each parent line for several generations until the desirable traits (intense red and disease resistance) are expressed consistently in each parent's offspring. At the end of these several generations, you save seeds from each parent line. All of the flowers in one parent line will be uniformly intense red, while those in the other are uniformly disease resistant.

At this point, you cross-pollinate the two parent lines. If you're lucky you'll create an intensely red-flowered, disease-resistant hybrid. Once this happens, you can continue to cross-pollinate your two pure parent lines year after year and produce consistent, high-quality hybrid seed every time.

Unfortunately, because of the painstaking, unpredictable nature of the process, hybrid seed tends to be more expensive than non-hybrid seed. However, measured against the results they produce, hybrid seeds often represent your best value.

Delphinium elatum ✳ Pacific Giant delphinium 'Astolat'

How should I plant perennial seeds in flats?

Jim ❖ Sow the seeds in rows 2 cm apart to avoid crowding. Crowded seedlings are difficult to successfully transplant, and are more vulnerable to damping off disease. Sow 4–7 seeds per cm of row (fine to medium–size seeds). Check the instructions on the packet to see if the seeds require light to germinate. If not, cover the seeds to a depth of twice their thickness.

My new perennials that I grew from seed from my original plant are not the same colour and size of flowers as the original. Why?

Jim ❖ Your plant may be a hybrid. Seeds taken from hybrid plants don't consistently grow "true to type." In other words, if you save hybrid seed and grow it the following year, some of the resulting plants will look like the parent, while others won't.

You're better off propagating hybrid plants through cuttings or division, rather than seed.

Rudbeckia hirta ❦ black-eyed susan

How do I store my seeds for next year?

Lois ❖ Seeds won't store forever. Some seeds have a very short shelf life, while others last a long time. I've had good results keeping seeds from columbine, pasque flower, martagon lily, and gasplant, to name a few.

I always store my seeds in an old Tupperware container, though any airtight container will do just fine. Throw in a packet of dessicant, store it in a cool, dark room, and you're set!

Jim ❖ Typically, germination rates decrease a few percentage points for every year that a seed is stored. Those seeds that do germinate may produce less vigorous plants. A properly stored seed not only germinates well when planted, but also produces a robust and healthy plant.

You can take certain steps to maximize the storage life of your seeds. For example, every 1% decrease in moisture content and every 5°C decrease in storage temperature (down to the freezing mark) doubles the shelf life (viability) of your seed. In other words, keep your seeds cool and dry. Never leave your seed packages open even for a short time—after only a few hours, the seeds begin to draw humidity from the air. Don't simply fold the tops of the packs over. Put them in airtight containers with a silica gel desiccant, and then store them in a cold room.

When to Transplant

When can I begin planting perennials?

Lois ❖ It depends on the region in which you live. I start putting perennials into the ground starting in mid to late April. Most perennials tolerate frost very well. Even the more sensitive ones (such as hostas) won't be severely injured by a frost and will bounce back quickly. If a hard frost is forecast, and you're a bit worried about some of your plants, just cover them with light fabric (an old sheet, for instance).

Jim ❖ Get out there as soon as you can work the soil! Perennials transplanted in cool spring weather suffer less stress and establish themselves more quickly. And if you shop for perennials early in the spring, you'll get the best selection.

How late can I plant perennials?

Lois ❖ You can plant container-grown perennials any time in the growing season, from early spring right up until the early fall. Provided you give your plants at least a few weeks to establish themselves, it's never too late!

Jim ❖ Again, perennials suffer less stress if you transplant them during cool weather. So long as you plant about three weeks before hard frosts, your perennials will do fine over the winter.

Garden centres rarely offer as wide a selection in the fall as they do in the spring. On the other hand, many offer their best sale prices at the end of the season.

What perennials are the most and least frost tolerant?

Lois ❖ As a rule of thumb, the earlier a plant emerges in the spring, the more frost tolerant it is. Plants that emerge later in the spring, such as hostas, can't take quite as much frost.

Jim ❖ Provided you can work the soil, you can plant most of your perennials. The soil protects plants' roots from freezing. Again, if you're worried about an impending hard frost, you can always cover your plants.

After I bring my perennials home, how long can I wait before planting them?

Lois ❖ Don't delay! Plant them as soon as possible. You can only afford to procrastinate for a short time. If you must leave your plants for a few days, make sure you don't allow the containers to dry out completely.

Jim ❖ Plant your perennials promptly. Otherwise, they'll rapidly outgrow their containers. You'll also have a difficult time keeping them properly watered.

I kept my perennials in my garage, and they've started to turn yellow. Have I done something wrong?

Lois ❖ I call this "garage-plant syndrome." Don't leave your plants in the garage! Put them into the ground as soon as you have the chance. If necessary, postpone shopping for perennials until you have time to plant them.

That said, if you can't plant them right away, be sure to put them outside during the day, and only put them back in the garage at night if temperatures are expected to drop below freezing. Inside a garage, even near a window, plants don't receive nearly enough light to maintain healthy growth.

Jim ❖ Outside, even on a cloudy day, your plants receive at least twice as much light as they do indoors in front of a bright, south-facing window. At the same time, the outdoor conditions help prepare plants for transplanting. Keeping your plants out of the garage is just as important as keeping your car out of the garden!

Ligularia wilsoniana ❧ rayflower

How to Transplant

How do I determine how far apart to set my plants?

Lois ❖ Check your plant's tag (or the seed packet, if you're growing from seed) to find how big the mature plants will be. Use that as a guideline when transplanting. Give each plant enough space so that a mature plant's leaves won't overlap with the plant beside it. Tightly crowded plants won't thrive and are more vulnerable to pests and disease.

How deep do I plant boxed perennials (bare-root perennials)?

Lois ❖ Just follow the directions on the package! In general, you plant the crown at soil level.

Jim ❖ The crown is the junction between a plant's roots and stem. With tender perennials, it's particularly important to protect the crown during a harsh winter. Generally speaking, if the crown dies, so does the plant.

Transplanting: step-by-step

1. Before you start planting, ensure that you know the mature size of each variety, so you can allow sufficient space between plants. If you have a garden plan, keep the drawing beside you. Plant the back row first.

2. Add 3–4 inches (7–10 cm) of organic matter to the soil surface. In hot, dry areas, add even more—an additional 2–3 inches (5–7 cm). Dig the organic matter in to about one spade's depth.

3. Each planting hole should be twice as wide and twice as deep as the size of the pot the plant is growing in. To aid root development, toss in a handful or two of bonemeal, and lightly stir it into the bottom of the planting hole.

4. Remove the plant from its pot. Gently untangle the rootball to enable roots to spread into the soil as the plant grows.

5. Refill the planting hole with fresh soil so the plant will be sitting at the same level as it was when growing in its pot. Stir the soil some more to mix the bonemeal into it. Now place the plant in the hole and firmly pack the soil around it, leaving a small depression around the base of the plant. Water until the soil is completely soaked.

6. New plants should be watered regularly and thoroughly twice a week for the first year after planting. Fertilize once a month with 20-20-20 until the first of August.

Dividing

How can I tell it's time to divide my perennials?

Lois ❖ Watch for these signs:

- The plant doesn't grow as large this season as it did in previous years.
- The centre of the plant is dead or weak.
- The plant appears crowded.
- The plant produces fewer and smaller flowers.

You say that spring is the best time to divide most perennials. What are the exceptions?

Jim ❖ Here are some of the main exceptions:

- peony – September
- bearded iris – August
- foxtail lily – September
- lily – September
- oriental poppy – August/September
- Early spring-blooming alpines and rock plants – after flowers have faded

How do I divide my perennials?

Jim ❖ It's actually fairly easy to divide perennials. Just follow these steps.

- Loosen the soil around the plant and carefully lift it out, including as much soil as possible.
- Divide the plant into two pieces (or three, if it's quite large), making sure that each piece has its own stem and root, and at least three to five vigourous shoots.

    Large perennials—Use a shovel to split the plant apart.

    Small perennials—Cut the plant into pieces with a sharp knife.

    Easily divided perennials—Gently pull the plant apart with your fingers.

- Use only the healthiest divisions for replanting, and discard the rest.
- Divisions from the outside edge of the clump tend to be the most vigourous; discard old, dead centres.
- Plant one part of the divided perennial in the original hole. Find other spaces in your garden for the rest of the pieces, or give them away to friends.
- Firm the soil around the plant, leaving a ring to trap and hold water.
- Finally, water and fertilize well with 10–52–10.

Iris germanica ❧ bearded iris 'Echo de France'

If I buy a plant with more than one stem, should I divide it now?

Lois ❖ You're better off planting it first, letting it establish itself, and then dividing it in a couple of years.

Jim ❖ Most perennials grow from root systems. Your new transplant hasn't had time to develop strong roots. You'll have much better luck if you wait a few years before dividing it.

Why do I need to divide some perennials (i.e., Morden mums) so frequently?

Lois ❖ Many perennials, including most mums, develop lots of branches and shoots. It doesn't take them long to become too dense.

Jim ❖ When plants become too dense, the shoots are forced to compete for sunlight, nutrients, and water. Shoots begin to turn yellow and die, particularly towards the plant's centre. It seems strange to think that you can invigorate a plant by cutting it in two, but it's true.

Moving Perennials

I'm moving. Can I take my perennials with me?

Lois ❖ A lot of people don't think twice before moving to a new house or a new city, but they hate the thought of leaving their gardens behind!

Don't try to move a large perennial. You may end up severely damaging the roots. If the plant is smaller and you can safely dig up its entire root system, you can move it any time up until 2–3 weeks before heavy fall frosts.

Otherwise, do your best to cultivate a friendly relationship with your house's new owners. That way, they won't object if you return in the spring to collect a few root divisions!

If I want to take root divisions with me, or give them away to friends, how should I transport them?

Jim ❖ Plant divisions in pots filled with lightweight, soilless potting mix, and keep them moist. Set them in a shady area outdoors until you're ready to plant. Never allow them to dry out.

Can I move my perennials in bloom?

Lois ❖ You can, but you shouldn't. This is the worst possible time to move plants.

Jim ❖ Plants in their reproductive phase (flowering) devote much of their energy to developing seeds, rather than developing food. During this particularly vulnerable stage, they cannot easily generate new growth. Avoid moving perennials in bloom, if at all possible.

Arisaema sikokianum
❦ dragonroot

Perennial Cuttings

Can I take cuttings from my perennials?

Jim ❖ It depends on the species.

- Some can be grown only from seed—e.g., Iceland poppy.
- Some are much more easily propagated by root division—e.g., blue fescue (*Echinacea*).
- Some produce bulblets—e.g., lilies.
- Some reproduce by basal shoots—e.g., mums.
- Some can be reproduced through cuttings; roots, stems, and tips—e.g., Oriental poppies.

What are tissue-cultured perennials?

Lois ❖ Traditional propagation methods are often very slow, making it difficult for growers and breeders to produce enough plants to sell. Tissue cultures accelerate the process.

Jim ❖ Tissue culture is the process of growing plants from tissues (callus) and organs (roots) in aseptic conditions. Often the tissue is taken from the plant's growing tip. A growing tip contains thousands of plant cells, each with the potential to grow into a new plant. This potential is called "totipotency." Researchers have been able to unlock the secrets of growing plants from tissue cultures with a combination of hormones and nutrients. Currently we grow the following plants from tissue cultures:

alum root *(Heuchera)*
pulmonaria *(Lungwort)*
primrose *(Primula)*
bleeding heart *(Dicentra)*
foam flower *(Tiarella)*
heartleaf forget-me-not *(Brunnera)*

CHAPTER 4 ❧
THE GROWING SEASON

The growing season is a time for regular maintenance. Weeding, watering, pinching—all of these activities are necessary to keep perennials looking beautiful.

But more importantly, the growing season is the time to sit back and enjoy your garden. Bob Stadnyk puts it this way: "Spend a little time each day just experiencing the plants. Watch them evolve over the course of the season, and enjoy their splendour. In a well-stocked perennial garden, there's always something new to see as the summer passes."

Spring

What should I do to my perennial beds in the spring?

Jim ❖ Here's a spring checklist for your perennial beds.

- Remove any mulch.
- Cut down and remove any debris from the previous year.
- Add compost or well-rotted manure around the plants.
- Remove any perennial weeds that have overwintered.
- Divide plants as necessary.
- Water thoroughly and fertilize.

When should I uncover my perennials?

Lois ❖ The best time to uncover perennials is when the buds swell on native trees and shrubs.

How do I remove mulch? Can it hurt the plants?

Jim ❖ It depends on the plant. Some perennials may have started to send flower buds and shoots up into the mulch. You might accidentally injure these plants if you're careless with your rake.

Gently remove the upper layer of mulch with the rake, and then use your hands for the lower layers. If you don't see any emerging shoots, you can rake away the remaining mulch.

It's early spring and my perennials are not coming up. Are they dead? How long do I wait before deciding to replace them?

Lois ❖ One May morning, a lady walked into our store with this massive clump of soil in a box. She said it was a dead hosta. I took the box, scratched away a bit of soil, and found about 30 emerging buds just coming up. I told her to go straight home and plant that hosta right away! This is one of the biggest mistakes we all make with perennials: not being patient enough. I always tell people to wait until June before digging up their plants.

Jim ❖ Even though the snow has melted and the air temperature has warmed up, the soil may still be relatively cool. Perennials respond to the temperature of the soil, not the air. It can take several weeks for the soil to warm sufficiently for growth to resume.

Not all perennials come up at the same time. Each plant variety has its own schedule. For instance, hostas are very slow to emerge in spring.

Location is another important factor. If your perennials are in a spot that's warmed by the sun, they'll emerge much more quickly than they would in shaded soil.

If June arrives and you still don't see any signs of life, it's time to go shopping for replacements.

My perennials are coming up too early. What do I do?

Lois ❖ In general, you can trust your plants. Your perennials are only responding to the overall weather.

Jim ❖ Sometimes, an early stretch of warm spring weather triggers perennials to emerge earlier than they should, particularly those planted on south-facing slopes. This rarely poses any long-term threat to your plants, but if you're really concerned you can pile up the snow or add a layer of mulch to slow plant emergence.

If temperatures dip well below freezing, you can cover your plants with old blankets. Some of the top growth might still be damaged, but your plants will be fine in the long run.

We've had a heavy snowfall, and some of my perennials had already emerged from the soil. What do I do?

Lois ❖ Don't worry. Just leave the snow there and allow it to melt naturally. Heavy snowfall may break the odd branch or flower, but it won't threaten the long-term health of your perennials. In fact, snow provides lots of moisture for the roots and insulates the plant from cold air.

Summer

Watering and Fertilizing

How often should I water my perennials?

Lois ✤ It varies so much from plant to plant that I can't give one answer. Some plants prefer moist soil, while others eventually die if you keep them wet.

Most varieties, once they're established, flourish with weekly waterings.

Jim ✤ Water new transplants every couple of days until they're well established. After that, a thorough soaking once per week is usually sufficient. During extended hot, dry spells you may need to water every three or four days.

What's the best way to water my perennials?

Lois ✤ I like to use a water wand with a good flood nozzle. It allows me to deliver the water right to the base of the plant, where it belongs.

Jim ✤ The biggest mistake that many gardeners make when watering is to sprinkle the leaves instead of soaking the plant's base. When you water deeply, you encourage your plants to develop deep root systems. This helps them cope with dry spells.

Use a flood nozzle and water around the base. Try not to soak the foliage, or you may promote diseases like grey mould and powdery mildew.

How can I tell if I'm overwatering my perennials?

Lois ❖ If the leaves of the entire plant begin to turn yellow, and the soil around it feels very wet, chances are it's waterlogged. Check your soil for proper drainage (see Soil, chapter 1), and allow the surface to dry out between waterings.

Why does my plant stay wilted even after I have watered it?

Lois ❖ The water may not have penetrated deeply enough into the soil, so that your plant is not absorbing any moisture.

Jim ❖ Several factors can prevent your plant from absorbing water properly.

- The water may not have penetrated deeply enough into the soil.

- On a very hot day, a newly planted perennial may transpire moisture more quickly than it can draw it up from the soil.

- Your plant may not have rooted into the garden soil properly. Often if a plant was rootbound before it was transplanted, the roots will be so tightly wrapped around themselves that they will resist the penetration of water. The soil surrounding the rootball will be wet but the roots themselves will be bone dry.

- If you inadvertently water the foliage, the weight of the water can temporarily bend the leaves down.

- Other root problems, for example root rot, also reduce your plant's ability to draw up moisture.

Pulsatilla vulgaris ❦ European pasque flower

I've heard that I should be careful when watering on sunny days, because water on the leaves can cause burning. Is this true?

Lois ❖ There's no truth at all to this popular myth. Water on leaves can, however, foster various diseases. Grey mould, for example, thrives on moist foliage. This is why I always recommend watering with a good flood nozzle, so that you can send all of the water to the soil around the base of the plant where it's needed.

Jim ❖ This myth simply refuses to die! Don't believe it!

Look at it this way: what would happen if water droplets really did burn leaves? A brief rainstorm followed by sunshine would burn every plant for miles around!

That said, it's still not a good idea to water during the heat of the day, because you lose too much moisture to evaporation. Water your garden first thing in the morning, to give your soil a chance to absorb as much of the water as possible.

When I water my containers, how do I know if they've been watered enough? Should the water be dripping out of the bottom?

Lois ❖ You've got to thoroughly soak the container each and every time. Don't just "baptize" your plants! Sprinkling a bit of water on the surface results in shallow, under-developed roots. You want the moisture to go right to the bottom. I like to water until I see water flowing from the bottom of the pot.

Jim ❖ Water your containers every time the soil surface begins to dry out. Assuming you have good potting soil, it's nearly impossible to overwater. Properly balanced soil retains the right amount of moisture and allows any excess to drain away. If your soil doesn't stay moist or if it becomes waterlogged, you should consider changing the soil. Be sure to use a professional potting mix with the right blends of wetting agents, peat moss, perlite, vermiculite and lime.

Over the years, our customers have experienced far more problems due to underwatering than overwatering. Overwatering is rarely an issue.

If I know a plant is drought tolerant, should I bother watering it?

Lois ❖ Remember what tolerant means. Just because a plant can withstand drought doesn't mean that it thrives in drought! Without water, even the toughest plants will eventually die. It is very important to water your plants regularly until they are well established—even those that are drought tolerant.

Jim ❖ Drought-tolerant plants don't like being constantly wet, so it's a good idea to allow the surface of the soil to dry out between waterings. Provided you get a good, soaking rain every few weeks, you might get by without watering your drought-tolerant plants. However, they definitely need your help during extended drought.

Some heavy feeders

lily
bearded Iris
clematis
Oriental poppy
  (Papaver orientale)
delphinium
monkshood (*Aconitum*)

Fertilizer

What fertilizer should I use?

Lois ❖ Fertilize new transplants once a week for three weeks with starter fertilizer (10-52-10), to promote vigorous roots and help your plants get established. After two or three weeks, switch to a good all-purpose (20-20-20) fertilizer once a month. Be careful not to over-fertilize. Most perennials don't feed as heavily as vegetables and annuals.

Jim ❖ Some gardeners rely almost entirely on compost and well-rotted manure, while others use granular or water soluble fertilizers. I prefer 20-20-20 or 15-15-30 once a month during the spring and summer. Stop fertilizing in early August, to allow your plants time to prepare for the winter.

That said, some perennials need more fertilizer than others. As a rule, shade perennials require much less fertilizer than sun perennials. You should adjust your fertilizing routine to the specific needs of your plants.

Some light feeders

trillium
astilbe
hosta
alpine plants
Siberian iris *(Iris sibirica)*
epimedium
hops
Maltese cross
  (Lychnis chalcedonica)

If I use slow-release fertilizer, should I add it in the spring or fall?

Lois ❖ I fertilize in the spring. Some people get excellent results from applying granular fertilizer in the late fall. However, be careful not to apply fertilizer too early in the fall. You may end up triggering new growth, making the plant more prone to winter injury.

Jim ❖ A perennial's roots begin to grow in the spring long before you see any sign of life above ground. By adding granular fertilizer in the fall, you give the roots a real jumpstart in the spring. However, if you fertilize too early in the fall, your plants may produce new foliage and risk winter injury. Apply granular fertilizer only after your plants are completely dormant (late October, early November).

Which works better, chemical or organic fertilizer?

Lois ❖ Both work equally well. As long as your plants get the nutrients they need, they don't really care how they get them. I like to use water-soluble fertilizers because they act so quickly and they are so easy to use, but many people achieve excellent results with fish fertilizers, kelp meal, manure teas, and even bat guano.

Jim ❖ All fertilizers are actually "chemical" fertilizers, in that they deliver the same elements and compounds to your plants. However, organic and non-organic fertilizers differ in the way they deliver these nutrients.

When you add manure to your soil, for example, microorganisms in the soil digest it, breaking it down into separate compounds such as ammonium, nitrates, phosphates, and iron oxides. Chemical fertilizers, such as 20-20-20, also contain ammonium, iron, phosphates, and so on. Unlike organic fertilizers, however, they don't have to be broken down before releasing nutrients to the plant. In either case, the plant eventually absorbs the same compounds in the same form, whether from an organic or non-organic source.

Keep in mind, however, that organic fertilizers provide more than short-term benefit to your plants. Because they take time to break down, they provide a long-term reservoir of nutrients in your soil. Manure, compost, and peat moss also improve your soil's texture and moisture retention.

Organic fertilizers generally have a low analysis (e.g., fish fertilizer is approximately 3-1-1), so you often need larger quantities to provide the same amounts of nutrients as a chemical fertilizer.

Organic Fertilizer: Manure

Why do gardeners add manure to their soil?

Lois ❖ Manure adds organic material to your soil. Make sure to use well-rotted manure, not fresh. Fresh manure burns your plants.

Jim ❖ Manure builds up the organic matter in the soil. It absorbs and retains nutrients and water, and provides a slow-release source of nutrients while greatly improving soil texture.

Does it matter what kind of manure I use (sheep, steer, etc.)?

Jim ❖ Manure does vary in composition somewhat from animal to animal (see following table), but you can use any type. Just remember to use well-composted manure; green manure is too rich and can burn perennial roots.

If you're using mushroom manure (usually horse manure that has been used for mushroom culture), be careful not to add too much. It contains very high levels of salts and can burn your plants. Don't add more than a 1-cm layer of mushroom manure, and be sure to mix it thoroughly into your soil.

Typical Composition of Manures

Source	Dry Matter (%)	Approximate Composition (% dry weight)		
		N	P_2O_5	K_2O
Dairy	15–25	0.6–2.1	0.7–1.1	2.4–3.6
Feedlot	20–40	1.0–2.5	0.9–1.6	2.4–3.6
Horse	15–25	1.7–3.0	0.7–1.2	1.2–2.2
Poultry	20–30	2.0–4.5	4.5–6.0	1.2–2.4
Sheep	25–35	3.0–4.0	1.2–1.6	3.0–4.0
Swine	20–30	3.0–4.0	0.4–0.6	0.5–1.0

Monarda didyma ❧ beebalm 'Petite Delight'

What is manure tea?

Lois ❖ I've never made manure tea, or compost tea, but a lot of people swear by it. Like the name suggests, it's a liquid fertilizer made by soaking manure or compost in water.

You brew it in much the same way as you would orange pekoe, but in a bigger pot! Just shovel some manure or compost into a burlap bag and tie it shut. Then immerse your "tea bag" into a large bucket or barrel of water, cover it, and leave it to steep for a few days. Before using the liquid on your plants, be sure to dilute it to a very light brown colour.

Use the tea in place of regular water. In my opinion, the amount of work in brewing this tea far outweighs the benefit to the plants, but don't let me stop you from giving it a try. I wouldn't use it on edible flowers, however, because of potential health problems.

Jim ❖ Keep a few points in mind when using manure or compost tea.

- Manure may contain plant diseases, and seedlings are especially susceptible.
- Manure teas may contain high levels of ammonia that can injure seedlings.
- Because tea is a weakened solution of manure, it may not contain enough nutrients for rapidly growing plants. Also, as with any manure, the composition varies depending on age and origin of the manure.
- Manure may contain disease organisms that could pose a human health risk.

Chemical Fertilizer: Composition

On fertilizer packages, what do the three numbers represent?

Jim ❖ The numbers refer to the percentage by weight of nitrogen—phosphate—potash in the fertilizer.

Nitrogen is crucial for leaf growth, phosphates promote strong root development, and potash aids in all-round plant health.

Do brand names matter, or is one 20-20-20 fertilizer like the next?

Jim ❖ The numbers represent a minimum chemical analysis, and no reputable company would try to shortchange you. The only differences might lie in the ease with which the fertilizer dissolves, the chemical formulation of each nutrient, and the composition of its inert ingredients. In general, though, you'll find that most 20-20-20 fertilizers work well in the garden.

Weeding

How can I minimize weeding?

Lois ❖ Minimize is the right word, because you'll never eliminate weeding entirely! Here are a few tips.

- Start off with a clean garden. Spend a full season if necessary to control weeds prior to planting (tillage, Roundup, etc.).
- Use only clean topsoil, compost, and manure.
- Never let annual weeds go to seed.
- Eliminate perennial weeds before they have a chance to become established.
- Add mulch to your flowerbeds.
- Use a weed barrier where practical.

Should I use weed barrier in my perennial bed?

Jim ❖ Yes, provided you don't have to cut too many holes in the fabric (this defeats the purpose because weeds can grow through). Be sure to make the holes big enough to allow the perennials to grow to their mature size.

Use a high-quality fabric; fewer weeds can grow through and it also tends to be more durable. You must remember to soak your perennials more thoroughly when watering because the fabric intercepts some of the moisture.

Finally, don't use weed barriers for perennials that spread.

What's the easiest way to pull weeds?

Lois ❖ If you weed a few days after a good rain, the weeds pull out of the soil more easily. It is much easier weeding after a rainfall than when the soil is dry. If you do find yourself weeding a dry bed, use a sturdy hoe to get around the leaves of the weed, and pull it up from its base. Be sure to add compost or peat moss every year to keep the soil soft and easy to weed.

Platycodon grandiflorus ❧ dwarf balloon flower 'Sentimental Blue'

How do I get rid of weed seeds in my soil?

Lois ❖ Always, always try to plant into clean soil! If it takes one or even two years to get rid of problem weeds, do it. It's worth the effort!

To eliminate a severe weed problem from your garden, keep it bare all summer. Rototill, hoe, or spray for weeds when necessary. Be very careful not to allow any weeds to go to seed. It's hard work, but it's the only way you'll be able to reduce your weed problem in the long run.

If you insist on planting a garden, try dividing your problem area in half. Plant one half of your garden, and treat the other half for weeds. Next year, switch sides.

Jim ❖ Here are my best tips for reducing your weed problem.

- Never allow the weeds to go to seed. A single pigweed can produce up to one million seeds each year!
- Perennial weeds that spread by rhizomes, such as quackgrass, require a rigorous, regular tillage program. You may have to till the soil weekly for an entire year to get rid of these persistent weeds. The best solution is to apply the herbicide glyphosate (commonly known as Roundup, Touch-down, Renegade, and a host of other names) when the perennial weeds are 15 to 20 cm tall.
- Don't introduce weeds into your garden in the first place—always buy clean potting or garden soils.
- Never plant into areas infested with tough-to-control weeds like thistle or quack grass—eliminate these weeds first.

Flowers

How can I get my perennials to rebloom?

Lois ❖ Most perennials bloom only once per season. Some bloom for longer periods if you remove each flower once it begins to fade.

There are exceptions to the rule. You can trick your Oriental poppies and delphiniums into blooming twice per season. Once the first set of flowers has finished, cut the plant back to a height of 15 to 30 cm, and add a high-phosphorus fertilizer (like 10-52-10). You should see a second flush of flowers later in the summer.

Jim ❖ Perennials, unlike most annuals, won't bloom continuously. They have definite blooming periods. To have a continuous show of colour, mix together varieties that bloom at different times of the growing season. You can also include a grouping of annuals, to provide a summer-long spot of colour while the perennials go in and out of bloom.

Should I cut off the flowers once they are finished? How far down do I cut?

Lois ❖ It's a good idea to remove spent blooms, unless you plan to save seed or you plan to use the seed pods in dried flower arrangements. If you allow the seed pods to ripen and shatter, you may end up with many tiny seedlings. Cut the flower stalks off down to the level of the leaves, and leave the leaves in place so that they can continue to produce food for the roots.

Jim ❖ By removing spent flowerheads, you allow your plants to devote more of their energy to developing leaves and roots, rather than producing seeds. Remember that you should let your biennals go to seed; otherwise, they won't return the next season.

Should I cut my plants back once they stop blooming? Will it hurt them?

Lois ❖ Don't cut a plant back just because it's no longer in bloom. The foliage continues to produce food for the plant as long as it's still green and growing.

Jim ❖ A perennial's chance of winter survival depends to a large extent on its carbohydrate reserves. Leaves produce carbohydrates that are stored in the perennial's roots and crown during the winter. Plants with inadequate carbohydrate reserves are much more prone to winterkill.

How can I get my plant to produce bigger flowers?

Jim ❖ Plants only perform up to their potential if you provide them with ideal growing conditions. Only those plants that receive ideal levels of sunlight, moisture, and nutrients reach their full potential and produce the biggest possible flowers. The right location and good soil are equally important.

You can also encourage bigger flowers by removing a few of the tiny, newly formed flower buds. This allows the plant to redirect energy to the remaining flowers. If you do this, you will often end up with larger flowers. However, you'll have fewer flowers overall, so it's a trade-off.

Fall

Should I cut back the foliage on my perennials in the fall?

Jim ❖ There are several advantages to cleaning up your perennial beds in the fall.

- The beds appear tidier throughout the fall and winter.
- There's less work to do next spring.
- You eliminate any disease-ridden foliage and reduce hiding places for insects to overwinter.
- You can amend the soil with compost or manure, rough digging it in between plants.
- You can divide those plants that require fall division (e.g., peonies, lilies, poppies).

However, you should not cut back any of the perennials you planted during the current growing season. And don't cut them back all the way to the ground: a little foliage can protect plants from winterkill by catching snow, which acts as an insulator.

Some perennials should never be cut back, including hostas, alpines, most rock-garden perennials, the succulents (eg., stonecrop, hens & chicks, yucca).

How can I tell that it's time to cut down my perennials?

Jim ❖ Don't cut your perennials down until frost has killed the tops. It's critical to allow leaves to continue producing energy for as long as possible. A perennial's vigour and winter survival depend on adequate energy reserves in the crown and roots.

Also, if you cut down a perennial too early it may try to grow back, especially if you have a warm fall. This depletes the plant's energy reserves at a critical time of year. The plant becomes weaker and more vulnerable to winter injury.

Which perennials have a tendency to go dormant and disappear or wither once they're finished blooming?

Lois ❖ The blue Himalayan poppy dies back in the summer heat. Since it's a big plant, you should fill in the space with another plant.

Jim ❖ Other perennials that go dormant in summer include fernleaf peony, shooting star, trillium, erythronium, and Oriental poppy.

Should I water my perennials in the fall?

Jim ❖ Yes. Dry soil can damage perennials. Give your plants a good soaking a few weeks before freeze-up. Water the area around the base of your plants, not the crowns themselves. Crowns can be damaged if they're too wet when the soil freezes.

Winter

Why didn't my perennial survive the winter?

Jim ❖ Here are the most common reasons why a perennial might fail to survive the winter.

- The plant is not hardy in that region.
- The plant dried out in early spring or during the winter, especially along the south wall of a house.
- The soil was waterlogged. Poor soil drainage is a leading cause of winterkill.
- Nitrogen fertilizer was applied too late in the season. Nitrogen stimulates soft growth, draining the plant's energy reserves at a time when it should be accumulating energy.
- An area has suffered an abnormally cold winter, with little or no snow cover.
- The plant was weak due to inadequate nutrient levels throughout the growing season.
- Pests or disease had weakened the plant.
- Temperatures dropped abruptly in the fall, before the plant had time to acclimatize.

Should I water my perennials during the winter if it thaws?

Jim ❖ Provided the soil hasn't completely dried out, don't worry about your perennials. If you do experience an extended spell of mild, dry weather, however, you should give your plants a midwinter drink. Just be sure to water only around the base, keeping the moisture off the crown.

Keep an especially close watch on any perennials planted against the south wall of your house. The soil there can dry out very quickly in warm weather.

I'm growing a perennial in a container. How do I overwinter it?

Jim ❖ The garden is the safest place for all your perennials. In the fall, move your plant to the garden and water it well. If you prefer, you can leave the plant in its container, planting the whole container in your garden to the level of the rim.

If you'd like to try preserving the entire plant, dig a trench, bury it sideways, and cover it with a thick layer of lightweight material like peat moss. Be sure to mark it at both ends so that you dig it up next spring.

Trillium cernuum ❧ nodding trillium

I grew some perennials in a planter. Can I overwinter them in the garage?

Jim ❖ You can give it a try, provided you have an unheated, well-insulated garage. The temperature should be consistent, and it should fall between -5 and 5° C.

Allow the plants to freeze down in the fall, then cut them back and put the planter in your garage. Once the average garage temperature drops down near the freezing mark, cover the planter with insulation. Water well before putting it in the garage. Check once a month throughout the winter for moisture and signs of sprouting. If the soil stays frozen, you may not need to add moisture at all, but if the soil begins to dry out, add some cold water.

Ironically, the biggest challenge with garages is not the cold, but the heat. If the soil temperature in the planter rises much above freezing (5°C or more) in midwinter, the perennials may begin to grow. It's very difficult to stop them from growing once they start. They tend to become severely weakened in the low-light environment of a garage.

In other words, this isn't a foolproof method. I recommend planting your perennials out in the garden (see previous question).

Paeonia ❧ Japanese peony 'Gay Paree'

Clematis ❀ hybrid clematis 'Nelly Moser'

Mulching

How do I know which perennials need to be mulched?

Jim ❖ Talk to other gardeners, consult staff at your garden centre, read books on perennials, and use a good zone map as a guide. You can't over-mulch, but you can under-mulch—so, if in doubt, mulch!

It's also a good idea to mulch any perennials planted during that year—especially those planted in the fall. Because their roots haven't grown very far into the soil, they're more likely to be heaved out of the ground by the alternating freezing and thawing in late fall and early spring.

How do I mulch?

Jim ❖ Mulch the crowns with at least 15 cm of dry peat moss and cover with plastic to keep the peat moss dry. You can also lay evergreen boughs or cornstalks over your perennials to help trap snow cover and hold finer mulch in place.

At the greenhouse, we overwinter some perennials outside in pots by covering them with an insulating blanket called microfoam, topped with 15 cm of peat moss and a thin layer of plastic to hold the peat moss in place. The temperature beneath the blanket stays just below the freezing mark, which is ideal.

When should I mulch?

Lois ❖ Mulch late in the season, three or four weeks after the last killing frost. If you mulch your plants too early, heat can build up beneath the mulch and the perennials will get accustomed to the warmth, making them more prone to winter injury.

I waited too long and my perennials are covered in snow. Will they survive? Should I scrape off the snow and mulch them?

Lois ❖ No, not necessarily. Snow is an excellent insulator. If the weather warms up and the snow melts, you can then apply mulch to your tender perennials. Otherwise, just leave the snow where it is, and add a few extra shovels full if you get the chance.

Scabiosa columbaria ❧ pincushion flower 'Pink Mist'

CHAPTER 5 🌸
ENJOY PERENNIALS

*Most people don't think of perennials as
a source for cutflowers, but a perennial
bouquet can be just as delightful as one
made of roses or annuals. Of course,
many perennials depend on having a few
flowers to set seed for next year, but there
are many you can cut without fear—as
long as you can bear to do it!*

Cutting

Can I use my perennials for cutflowers?

Lois ❖ Certainly! You can cut flowers from just about any perennial, although some are better suited for cutting than others. I look for plants with showy blooms and strong stems—these generally look better and last longer.

The table opposite lists some of my favourite perennial cutflowers.

Jim ❖ Leave your plants untouched for the first year after planting, to allow them to become established. After that, try to remove as little foliage as possible when you cut flowers. Remember, leaves produce nutrients, so if you remove too many of them you weaken the plant.

How far down the stem can I cut flowers for indoors?

Lois ❖ It depends on the size of the plant. You may prefer nice, long stems, but if you remove too much foliage you risk damaging your plant's health. Here are some rough guidelines for some of the most popular perennial cutflowers.

- phlox – 30 to 60 cm
- peony – 30 to 60 cm
- lily – 60 to 90 cm
- monkshood – 60 to 90 cm
- lily-of-the-valley – 10 cm
- iris – 40 to 60 cm
- baby's breath – 30 to 45 cm
- delphinium – 45 cm to 1 m.

When is the best time of day to cut flowers from my perennials?

Lois ❖ Cut them in the cool of the morning (before 10 am), when the flowers are cool.

Jim ❖ Blossoms lose moisture rapidly during the heat of the afternoon. If you cut them in the morning or evening, they're under much less heat stress. If the soil is on the dry side, thoroughly water your garden at least a few hours before cutting flowers, to ensure that the blooms contain as much moisture as possible.

How can I make my cutflowers last longer?

Jim ❖ In addition to cutting your blooms in the morning, here are a few other tips.

- High bacteria populations in your water can plug the stems and cause the flowers to wilt. To reduce bacteria numbers, rinse your vase thoroughly with a bleach solution to sterilize it, then rinse it again with plain water to remove the bleach residue.

- Before putting the flowers in your vase, re-cut the stems. Always cut the stems underwater to avoid embolisms (trapped air bubbles that prevent water flow within the stems).

- Cut the stems at a 45° angle. This exposes a greater surface area to the water and keeps the ends off the bottom of the vase, allowing the stems to draw water more easily.

- Cut off any foliage that will be below the waterline to prevent rotting. Rotting vegetation produces ethylene gas, a plant hormone that causes flowers to drop. At the same time, decay also promotes rapid bacterial growth.

- Add floral preservative to supply sugar and prevent bacterial growth.

- Keep your flowers in a cool location, away from direct sunlight.

Lilium ❧ LA Hybrid Lily 'Royal Sunset'

Best perennials for cutting

aster (*Aster*)
astilbe (*Astilbe*)
baby's breath
   (*Gypsophila*)
bellflower (*Campanula*)
blue sage (*Salvia*)
coreopsis (*Coreopsis*)
delphiniums (*Delphinium*)
false sunflower (*Heliopsis*)
foxglove (*Digitalis*)
foxtail lily (*Eremurus*)
garden mums
   (*Dendranthema*)
garden phlox
   (*Phlox paniculata*)
globeflower (*Trollius*)
globe thistle (*Echinops*)
goldenrod (*Solidago*)
iris (*Iris*)
Joe Pye (*Eupatorium*)
lily (*lilium*)
lily-of-the-valley
   (*Convallaria majalis*)
lupine (*Lupinus*)
Maltese cross
   (*Lychnis chalcedonica*)
monkshood (*Aconitum*)
obedient plant
   (*Physostegia*)
ornamental onion
   (*Allium*)
peony (*Paeonia*)
pink (*Dianthus*)
Russian sage (*Perovskia*)
Shasta daisy
   (*Leucanthemum*)
showy daisy (*Erigeron*)
Helen's flower (*Helenium*)
soapwort (*Saponaria*)
speedwell (*Veronica*)
statice (*Limonium*)
yarrow (*Achillea*)

Drying

How do I air-dry perennial flowers?

Lois ❖ Choose flowers that haven't quite fully bloomed. I like to pick at 10 am or so, before the sun causes the flowers to open more fully. Tie the stems in loose bunches and suspend them upside-down in a dark, well-ventilated room. They should dry completely in a week or so, depending on the size of the blooms.

Jim ❖ Air-drying is the simplest and cheapest method, but the results can be mixed. Some colours may fade or darken, and some blooms won't retain their natural shapes well when air-dried.

Which perennials are best for drying?

Lois ❖ You can dry any kind of flower with silica gel. Look for blooms that have opened, but aren't yet fully blown—that is, past their prime. Flowers that are too old often continue to develop after you pick them, and you may wind up with a dried flower that falls to seed. Many flower buds also look lovely when dried. Pick the flowers mid morning, just after the dew has dried from the petals.

My friend dries flowers using silica gel. Where do I get it, and how do I use it?

Lois ❖ Blooms dried in silica gel retain their natural shape and colour much better than those that are air-dried. You can purchase silica gel at any good craft store and some garden centres.

Pour a thick bed of gel in the bottom of a box or other container. Lay the individual flowers on the gel, and gently pour more gel around and over them until they're completely buried. Leave them for 5-7 days, then check them carefully to confirm that they have dried completely.

Best perennials for drying

astilbe (*Astilbe*)
baby's breath (*Gypsophila*)
blanket flower
    (*Gaillardia grandiflorum*)
blue oat grass
    (*Helictotrichon
    sempervirens*)
    seed heads
blue sage (*Salvia*)
clematis (yellow bell)
delphinium (*Delphinium*)
evening primrose
    (*Oenothera*)
false sunflower (*Heliopsis*)
globe thistle (*Echinops*)
goldenrod (*Solidago*)
iris (seed pods)
masterwort (*Astrantia*)
moor grass (*Molinia*)
    seed heads
obedient plant
    (*Physostegia*)
    seed pods
ornamental onion
    (*Allium*)
peony (*Paeonia*)
Russian sage (*Perovskia*)
sage (*Artemisia*) (foliage)
sea holly (*Eryngium*)
shooting star
    (*Dodecatheon*)
statice (*Limonium*)
thyme (for miniature
    arrangements)
yarrow (*Achillea*)

Solidago sp. ✦ goldenrod 'Crown of Rays'

Jim ✦ Dessicants, such as silica gel, absorb and hold water molecules. That's why your flower dries out when you bury it in silica, even though there's virtually no air movement.

If you combine the silica-gel method with microwaving, your flowers will dry much more quickly. Bury the flowers in silica and then microwave them, box and all, for a minute or so (you'll have to experiment to find the exact times for your particular oven). Take the box out, and leave it undisturbed for half an hour. Then carefully check the petals to make sure they're papery-dry.

You can reuse silica gel almost indefinitely. If it ever loses its effectiveness, simply heat it in a warm oven for an hour or so to evaporate all the moisture.

Silica gel is an irritant to mucous membranes of the respiratory tract, so work in a well-ventilated area to avoid breathing in the dust. It's also a good idea to use gloves and eye protection to keep the dust away from your skin and eyes.

Eating

Are any perennials edible?

Some edible perennials

beebalm (*Monarda*)
   leaves, flowering tops
catmint (*Nepeta mussini*)
   roots, leaves
daylily (*Hemerocallis*)
   young roots,
   flowerbuds,
   expanded flowers
evening primrose
   (*Oenothera*)
   young shoots
goutweed (*Aegopodium*)
   young leaves
hollyhock (*Alcea*)
   young leaves, flowers
honeysuckle (*Lonicera*)
   young leaves
meadowsweet
   (*Filipendula*) flowers
ostrich fern (*Matteuccia*)
   young shoots
pink (*Dianthus*) flowers
primrose (*Primula*)
   flowers, young leaves
Shasta daisy
   (*Leucanthemum*) leaves
sweet rocket (*Hesperis*)
   flowers, leaves
yarrow (*Achillea*) young
   leaves, flowers
   (eat in moderation)
violet (*Viola*) flowers
wintergreen (*Gaultheria*)
   berries

Lois ❖ Absolutely! Some are obviously edible—vegetables such as asparagus, horseradish, rhubarb and Jerusalem artichoke are perennials. However, many perennials normally thought of as strictly ornamental can also be eaten.

Jim ❖ For example, daylily (*Hemerocallis*) flowers, flowerbuds, and young roots can all be eaten.

However, with many plants it's very important to know exactly what species you have before you try eating it. A plant part that may be edible on one particular species may be inedible on a different, closely related species.

Primula denticulata ❧ drumstick primrose

CHAPTER 6 🦋
TROUBLESHOOTING
PERENNIALS

I've yet to experience a trouble-free gardening season. There's always going to be a sudden bug infestation or a bothersome disease to put a crimp in your plans—but sometimes that's part of the fun. Trying out your Baba's old pest-control methods can be a way to connect with the past, and there's nothing like the thrill of saving your plants from powdery mildew thanks to some newly gleaned knowledge.

"Take a closer look at your perennials, and do it more often," Bob says. "That way you don't always have to resort to pesticides. Sometimes pinching off a diseased leaf is all it takes to forestall a disaster, if you catch it quickly enough."

Insects

How can I minimize insect problems in my garden?

Lois ❖ You'll never be able to avoid bugs entirely, but you're always better off if you catch a problem early. I take a good look at my plants every time I visit my garden. If I see a few bugs, I squish them. If I spot some aphids, I grab my spray bottle of insecticidal soap.

Jim ❖ Insects and diseases often strike plants that are stressed. If you keep your garden clean and give your plants proper care, you'll avoid many problems.

If you constantly have a disease problem in one part of your garden, you might consider replacing your plants with a more resistant species (often, you can even find a disease-resistant variety of the same species).

Which perennials are vulnerable to cutworms?

Jim ❖ Cutworms can attack the soft, young growth on nearly any perennial, but they rarely cause any long-term damage to them.

There is a saliva-like substance on the leaves of my plant. What causes this and how can I prevent it?

Jim ❖ The "saliva" is likely a foamy substance secreted by an insect called a spittlebug. The foam protects the spittlebug from predators. Spittlebugs seldom cause any major health problems on perennials, but the foam does look unsightly. The simplest approach is to wash off the foam with a stream of water. If you're persistent, you can permanently wash the bugs off the plant as well.

Spittlebugs have a fondness for perennials with lots of leaves, but they're not particular—any perennial may be vulnerable.

What can I do about the green worms that eat my delphinium, monkshood, and columbines?

Lois ❖ If there aren't too many, just pick them off. If you've got a more severe problem, you may have to use a systemic insecticide like Latox.

Jim ❖ The green worm is the larval stage of moth called a leaf tier. The caterpillar ties up a mass of silk and leaves to protect itself. The leaf tier feeds on native larkspur which belong to the delphinium family. Ornamental delphiniums are very similar to larkspur, so the leaf tier feeds on wild or garden varieties with equal zeal.

Try this: when your plants get to be about 30 cm tall (usually in early May), cut them back. The bugs will be in their feeding cycle, but they'll have nothing to eat. By the time your plants regrow, the bugs will have passed their feeding stage.

What do slug eggs look like?

Jim ❖ Look for small, round, translucent eggs in small clusters in the soil. Some slug species lay 500 eggs per year. A pelletized slow-release fertilizer called osmocote (sprinkled on the soil surface of containerized shrubs) is sometimes mistaken for slug eggs.

You can destroy many slug eggs by tilling the soil thoroughly.

How can I discourage slugs?

Lois ❖ If you get a lot of slugs in your garden, you can try planting slug-resistant perennials. In general, slugs hate any plant with a bristly or hairy surface.

Jim ❖ Try not to give them places to hide. Slugs love to lurk in moist, shady spots—under decks, rock piles, railway ties, etc. Keep your yard free of debris and slugs will have no place to lurk.

If you have a lot of slugs, Safer's Slug and Snail Bait controls them organically. You can also use any slug bait that has metaldehyde as an active ingredient. Metaldehyde can be poisonous to animals, though, so place it in a container that is inaccessible to pets.

My yard seems to have become instantly infested with aphids. Where did they all come from?

Jim ❖ Aphids really do seem to come out of nowhere! Some aphid species lay eggs on tree trunks in the fall. These hatch once the weather warms in the spring. Other aphid species can literally "blow in," riding the winds from the Gulf of Mexico.

Aphids reproduce very rapidly, especially during warm, dry weather. They are parthenogenetic, meaning that the females don't require males in order to produce offspring. During the summer aphids give birth to live young, not eggs, making reproduction that much quicker.

There are many different species of aphids: green peach aphid, foxglove aphid, melon aphid, and honeysuckle aphid, to name just a few.

How do I get rid of aphids?

Jim ❖ You'll never get rid of all the aphids in your garden, but you can take steps to control their numbers. The key is to catch the problem early. High aphid populations are difficult to control with any method.

When you spot aphids, spray affected plants with insecticidal soap, making sure not to miss the undersides of the leaves. Insecticidal soap causes little damage to aphid predators like lacewings and ladybugs.

You can also try to attract more ladybugs to your garden, since they prey on aphids. Ladybug lures are available at most garden centres.

The retired fellow living next door uses rhubarb spray to fight aphids. Does this work?

Jim ❖ I've never tried it, but quite a few organic gardeners claim that homemade rhubarb spray kills aphids and other harmful insects. To make it, they steep rhubarb leaves in boiling water, strain the liquid, and add a dash of liquid soap.

Rhubarb leaves contain a very bitter-tasting toxic chemical called calcium oxalate. This is likely the active ingredient in your neighbour's spray. Exercise caution in handling and storing it. The solution is poisonous, so make sure you label the container to prevent people from accidentally drinking it.

Rhubarb spray is only one example of many homemade concoctions used by organic gardeners. Remember, though, that just because a product is "organic" doesn't mean it's safe. Judge each pest-control product based on its own merit.

The flowers on my salvia are brown and distorted, and open very slowly. What's wrong?

Jim ❖ It sounds as if you've got thrips in your garden. Thrips are very tiny, needle-shaped insects that love the pollen in flowers. They attack a wide variety of perennials. When they feed, they distort the flowers and can also cause the buds to turn brown.

The best way to check for thrips is to do the "tap test." Break off a flower bud from one of your afflicted plants and tap it sharply several times on a white sheet of paper. If any thrips fall out, you'll easily spot them scrambling across the paper.

Thrips are particularly attracted to yellow and blue flowers, so watch for them if you have perennials that sport these colours.

I used Diazinon on my beebalm for thrips and it didn't work. What should I be using?

Jim ❖ A single "blanket" spray of any pesticide is seldom effective on thrips. You must make several applications, especially if the thrips have entered the flowers, where they are well protected.

In any case, Diazinon isn't your best choice for treating thrips. Chlorpyrifos is more effective than Diazinon in treating thrips. Spray first with a pyrethoid insecticide (this irritates the thrips and flushes them out into the open). Then spray with chloropyritos. Typically, you'll have to spray three times, with five to seven days between applications.

My bamboo is losing its leaves. The fallen leaves are dry and curled up. Some of them have tiny spiderwebs on them. Why?

Lois ❖ Your bamboo is infested with spider mites, one of the most destructive pests in the garden. Spider mites attack many perennials, especially grasses and perennials growing in dry locations. Spider mites draw the sap out of the underside of leaves. Left unchecked, they can completely defoliate a plant in a few weeks. Spider mites prefer hot, dry weather, so watch for them during extended warm spells.

Jim ❖ If you keep a close lookout, you can catch a spider-mite problem at an early stage. If you spot spider mites, give your perennials a good spray with your garden hose, paying special attention to the undersides of the leaves. Insecticidal soap also helps clear up small spider-mite populations. Remember that the soap spray must contact the bugs, so you need to be thorough. Spider-mite eggs resist insecticides, so you should spray three times at weekly intervals to kill the mites as they hatch.

Pulmonaria saccharata ❧ Bethlehem sage 'Excalibur'

Animals

How do I keep animals out of my flowerbeds?

Jim ❖ Stout, sturdy fencing keeps out dogs and some wildlife. Cacti and sharp rocks discourage many animal pests. You can buy animal repellents at many garden centres and pet stores. You might also consider buying a motion-activated sprinkler.

If cats use your garden as a litter box, it may be that you're providing the perfect conditions. Water frequently, and at odd times, and the cats won't find your flowerbeds quite so comfy.

Will any perennials keep cats out of my yard?

Jim ❖ The foliage of salvia—especially 'May Night'—actually smells like cat urine. This normally might not be considered a desirable feature in a plant, but if roaming cats plague your garden it might help solve your problem. Jan Goodall, who works at our greenhouse, says that her own cats won't go near the stuff.

If that doesn't work, you may be able to keep cats out of your yard by buying each of your neighbours a catnip plant!

Other

My plants are turning yellow and going limp. What could be causing this?

Lois ❖ It sounds as if your soil is waterlogged. Be careful not to overwater your perennials—most perennials only need extra water during extended dry spells. If you're not watering too frequently, you may need to improve your soil's drainage by adding organic matter.

Perennials that deer typically don't eat

aster
beardtongue
beebalm
bishop's hat
black-eyed susan
blanke tflower
bleeding heart
catmint
daylily
foxglove
lupine
meadowsweet
monkshood
sage
Shasta daisy
snow-in-summer
spurge
white archangel
yarrow

Jim ❖ You can determine if drainage is the problem by grabbing and squeezing a handful of your moist soil. If it compacts into a muddy, clay–like ball, your soil probably has inadequate drainage.

Properly drained soil allows excess water to pass through, leaving tiny air spaces. If this doesn't happen, the roots become waterlogged. They can't adequately absorb oxygen and begin to die. Above ground, this translates into yellow, wilted foliage.

If you're growing your plants in containers, ensure that the pots all have drainage holes.

Perennials that rabbits typically don't eat

cactus
foxglove
gas plant
lily-of-the-valley
monkshood
sage
spurge
St. John's wort
stonecrop
thyme
yarrow
yucca

Sedum sp. ❧ stonecrop 'Matrona'

Some perennials for hot, dry spots

baby's breath
bitterroot
blanket flower
blue fescue
blue sage
cactus
coneflower
cornflower
daylily
fleeceflower
foxtail lily
gas plant
globe thistle
hens & chicks
hops
gay feather
cinquefoil
Russian sage
sage
salvia
sea holly
silver sage
snow-in-summer
soapwort
spurge
St. John's wort
stonecrop
yarrow
yucca

I've just watered my beds, but my plants are still wilting. What's wrong?

Jim ❖ Many problems can lead to wilting, but here's a lineup of the usual suspects.

• The plants haven't been watered thoroughly enough. You should soak the entire root zone every time you water.

• The plants are newly transplanted and the roots haven't grown into the soil. The moisture in the root ball is being pulled away by the dryer surrounding soil.

• Root rot has taken hold, and the diseased roots can no longer supply the leaves with enough moisture on warm days. If your soil is consistently too wet, this may be the problem.

• The soil is high in salts, and the plant roots are unable to draw in the salty solution.

My clematis is very dry beside my house. It's a white stucco house with mirrored windows.

Jim ❖ Plants grown in direct sun along a south-facing wall or fence receive an awful lot of heat and light. White or mirrored surfaces increase this effect. Vines also have a tough time thriving under eavestroughs, where they don't get any moisture. In areas like this, stick to perennials that can withstand extreme conditions.

Jan Goodall suggests that if you grow clematis on a lattice that's just 4 or 5 cm away from the siding, the reflected heat will be cut down so much that the plants won't suffer at all. "I also make anyone who buys a clematis from me promise to water it and to amend poor soil by adding lots of organic matter," she says. "Clematis won't grow if you plant them in clay and forget to water them."

Why didn't I get many blooms this year?

Jim ❖ Some perennials won't bloom until they've reached a certain size or leaf number. Newly planted perennials usually need a season or two before they begin to produce flowers.

Several other factors may also have prevented your perennials from blooming well this year. If your plants are in the wrong location, they might not be receiving enough light to produce blooms. You should also check your plants carefully for pest problems, such as aphids or thrips. It's also possible that you haven't fertilized enough—or perhaps you've added lots of manure, which promotes foliage growth but not flowering. Finally, your perennial may need to be divided.

Clematis ❀ hybrid clematis 'Carnaby'

I have valerian and catmint seeds sprouting all over the place. How can I prevent this problem?

Lois ❖ Never let your plants go to seed. Once the flowers begin to fade, cut them off and compost them before the seeds mature.

What is that white film on my phlox? I think it's killing it.

Lois ❖ That white stuff is likely a fungal disease called powdery mildew. It looks like talcum powder sprinkled across the leaves. Treat it right away—it spreads quickly.

Jim ❖ There are many different species of powdery mildew. Whatever the species, though, powdery mildew is a nasty, persistent threat to your plants. Fortunately, new mildew-resistant perennial varieties have already been developed, and more are appearing every day. Try growing the Flame series of phlox—one of the new resistant varieties.

How does powdery mildew spread?

Jim ❖ The mildew typically begins as a very tiny spore that lands on your leaf. It remains dormant until it gets the moisture it needs for germination. Once the leaf gets moist and stays moist for about three hours (say, from overhead sprinkling or condensation on a cool, moist night), the mildew begins to develop. It rapidly spreads in white strands (hyphae) across the face of the leaf, dropping pegs (haustoria) into the leaf to anchor it and allow it to draw nutrients from your plant. At that point, it doesn't need any more leaf-surface moisture to proliferate—it can get all it needs directly from within the leaves.

Powdery mildew tends to attack plants that are already vulnerable for one reason or another. Anything that weakens the plant allows the mildew to penetrate the leaf surface more easily. For instance, plants that don't get enough sunlight tend to have thinner leaves, making them more prone to infection. Plants deficient in nutrients (calcium in particular) have weaker leaf-cell walls and are also more vulnerable. Powdery mildew also often attacks plants stressed by drought.

How do I treat powdery mildew?

Jim ❖ Once powdery mildew takes hold, it is very difficult to control—in fact, I have yet to find a spray that can cure a badly infected plant. Your best bet is preventive action.

Spray susceptible plants before you even see the first sign of mildew. Spray every seven to ten days using benomyl. Some people also like to use baking soda: about 15 ml per 4 L of water (1 tablespoon per gallon) combined with a 10% solution of summer plant oil. Always experiment on a few leaves before treating the whole plant, to ensure the spray does no damage. Perennials vary considerably in their sensitivity to oil sprays.

Which perennials are prone to powdery mildew?

Jim ❖ Perennials that are particularly prone to powdery mildew include yarrow, columbine, aster, coreopsis, delphinium, lupine, beebalm, phlox, and speedwell.

Lunaria biennis ❧ money plant

Why isn't my plant blooming? I bought the large size to make sure I'd get blooms this year.

Jim ❖ There are several possible explanations.

- Your plant may be in too shady a location.
- The plant may have already finished blooming before you purchased it.
- You may be using the wrong type of fertilizer. Fertilizer too rich in nitrogen (e.g., lawn fertilizer) promotes foliage growth at the expense of blooms.
- Your plant may still need another year to mature before blooming.

Delphinium elatum ❧ Pacific Giant delphinium 'Guinevere'

Why do some of my perennials flop over even though they shouldn't need staking?

Jim ❖ If a plant doesn't get enough sunlight, its stem won't develop enough strength to support the plant's weight. Also, if a plant receives too much nitrogen from overfertilization or excessive compost, it will "lodge" (flop over). Fertilizers high in potash (i.e., with a high third number) tend to increase stem strength.

Your plants may also be spaced too closely. Before you plant perennials in your garden, find out how far apart each plant should be planted.

The leaves on my plants are yellowing. Am I overwatering?

Jim ❖ If only the lower leaves are yellow, then your plant is likely suffering from a shortage of nitrogen. Apply some all-purpose fertilizer (such as 20-20-20) and the problem should clear up.

If all the foliage has yellowed, you may indeed be overwatering. Overly dry soil or disease can also cause yellowed leaves.

Asperula gussoni ❧ lilac woodruff

Over the winter the plants along my driveway and sidewalk died. Why is this? Is there a plant that might work in this location?

Jim ❖ Do you use salt on your driveway in the winter? Most plants won't tolerate high salt levels. It's also possible that you may not have watered your plants well in the late fall.

During the winter, shovel some extra snow over these plants to protect and insulate them.

For challenging areas like these, you should try planting ruggedly hardy varieties such as stonecrops, poppies, peonies, cornflowers, and St. John's wort.

Dendranthema x *morifolium* ❧ Morden mum 'Cameo'

CHAPTER 7 🌿
PERENNIAL VARIETIES

*Perennials can appeal to—or repulse—
all of the senses. Beebalm foliage cries out
to be caressed, while chameleon plants
smell so bad that one of our more sensitive employees got sick after working with
them. There's an awful lot of variety in
the perennial world: Bob carries 5,000
different perennials in his
department, and that's just scratching
the surface of their diversity.*

*Sometimes a general solution isn't
enough, and variety-specific care is
required. Dividing your old irises may
rejuvenate them, but trying the same
thing on clematis will kill the plant.
It's worth any perennial lover's while
to take the time to learn a little
about their favourite varieties.*

General

I have two perennials of the same variety growing right next to each other. One is doing fine, but the other looks terrible. What's wrong?

Jim ❖ When grown from seed, plants of a single variety can vary considerably in form—much like human siblings, they can have significantly different genetic makeups. Plants grown from cuttings, on the other hand, are genetically identical (clones). If grown under similar conditions, they usually grow to be nearly identical to one another.

There are other possible explanations. One of the plants may have a disease or another problem that isn't readily apparent.

Also, drainage and available moisture can vary widely even when plants are relatively close together—especially near a house or garage.

Gaillardia grandiflorum ❧ blanket flower 'Baby Cole'

Aster novi-belgii ❦ aster 'Winston Churchill'

I would like to grow some native perennials. Can you recommend some?

Lois ❖ Every region has its own assortment of native perennials. Some of the nicest in my area include wild blanket flower (*Gaillardia aristata*), Canada violet (*Viola rugulosa*), early blue violet (*Viola adunca*), Canada anemone (*Anemone canadensis*), and pasque flower (*Pulsatilla patens*).

Jim ❖ More and more people these days prefer a wild, natural look for their gardens. Any good garden centre will be able to recommend suitable varieties for your particular area. Perennial wildflowers for other regions in North America include trillium, tiger lily, shooting star, and prairie smoke *(Geum triflorum)*.

Aster

The blooms on my asters are damaged by frost each fall before they have a chance to bloom. What can I do to encourage to bloom earlier?

Jim ❖ Some aster varieties don't bloom until late fall. You may have simply planted a variety that isn't appropriate for your local climate.

If several seasons have come and gone with no blooms, replace your asters with varieties that bloom earlier. For instance, New York aster (*Aster novi-belgii*) and New England aster (*Aster novae-angliae*) both bloom in late summer. Similarly, fall mums are available in three different blooming categories: early, mid, and late.

Astilbe x *arendsii* ❧ astilbe 'Cattleya'

Astilbe

Why won't my astilbes bloom?

Lois ❖ They might still be too young. Astilbes need time to get established before they'll bloom profusely.

Astilbes also won't bloom well if they get too much sun, or not enough moisture or fertilizer. Also, remember to plant them out of the wind. Finally, perhaps you've planted them too deeply. The eyes should be only about 1 cm beneath the surface.

Why does the foliage on my astilbe plants turn brown and dry in the summer?

Lois ❖ The leaves of astilbe quickly turn brown if you allow the soil to dry out. Wind can also injure them, drying their leaves to a crisp. To eliminate this problem, plant them in a semi-shaded, sheltered spot and keep the soil consistently moist.

Baby's Breath

Can I move my baby's breath once it's well established?

Lois ❖ No. Baby's breath usually dies if you try to divide or move it. It has a long, thick taproot that's difficult to dig up properly.

Bleeding Heart

My bleeding hearts are looking wretched. Can I prune them back a bit?

Lois ❖ Certainly. Go ahead and clean them up. Pruning the plant promotes new growth and opens the plant up to receive more sunlight.

Dicentra spectabilis ❧ common bleeding heart

Opuntia fragilis ❧ brittle prickly pear cactus

Cactus

Do cacti survive outdoors in Canada?

Lois ❖ Yes. In fact, several species are native to Canada. The brittle prickly pear (*Opuntia fragilis*) grows on the prairies, in parts of Ontario and well up into the Peace River country of northern Alberta and northern BC. And if you're travelling through the southern prairies, keep an eye out for *Coryphanta vivipara*, the native pincushion cactus. In the summer, it has lovely rose-pink flowers.

Jim ❖ Cacti love hot days and cool nights. In fact, many need cool nights in order to survive. Few cacti do well in regions where there's little difference between daytime and nighttime temperatures.

Chrysanthemum

How do I propagate chrysanthemums from stem cuttings?

Lois ❖ Here's one method.

- Select firm side shoots, 9–10 cm long.
- Dip each cutting in a rooting compound and shake off any excess.
- Insert the cut end into a pot filled with moist, pasteurized potting mix, and cover with a plastic bag to reduce moisture loss.
- Leave the bag in a bright spot (but not in direct sun).
- Check often for moisture and add water as needed.
- Once the roots are several centimetres long (which takes about 3 to 4 weeks), transplant the cuttings into pots and begin fertilizing them weekly with 10-52-10.

Clematis

How do I propagate clematis from cuttings?

Lois ❖ You can propagate clematis using the same method I described for chrysanthemums (p. 103).

Is there a hardy clematis that produces large flowers?

Lois ❖ *Clematis viticella* is very showy. The 'Polish Spirit' closely resembles 'Jackmanii' (the most popular hybrid), but is much hardier—it will easily survive in zone 3 and will often thrive in zone 2 with the proper winter protection. It produces large, dark-purple flowers.

Why do I have to plant hybrid clematis against my house?

Jim ❖ The walls radiate heat from the house, collect and reflect heat from the sun, and offer some protection from the wind. At the same time, heat from the basement warms the soil slightly during the winter. These factors combine to create a microclimate against the walls of your house, allowing you to successfully grow plants that might not normally be hardy in your climate—like hybrid clematis. It's also much easier to secure a trellis to the house, rather than support it out in the open.

Why does my clematis bloom only at the top?

Jim ❖ It's likely just the natural flowering habit for that particular variety. Many clematis species produce almost all of their blooms on new growth only. It's best to leave it alone, but if you like you can try cutting back the old wood to ⅔ of its size. This will help the plant to branch out, increasing the possibility of more blooms—though they will probably still be near the top of the vine.

What is clematis wilt? What causes it? Are there any preventative measures?

Jim ❖ Clematis wilt is most often caused by a fungus, *Ascochyta clematidina,* which may attack any part of the plant from the crown up but typically infects the stem near the soil. The fungus eventually girdles the stem, causing the foliage to wilt. The infection often begins from spores on the stumps of old stems.

You can save some of your plants by always planting clematis crowns 2 cm below soil level. That way, if the fungus destroys all of the top growth, the crown will remain healthy and be able to send up new growth. Copper-based sprays can also help prevent the problem. If you've had clematis wilt in your garden in the past, apply a copper-based spray to your vines every two weeks early in the growing season.

If clematis wilt does kill your plant entirely, do not plant a new clematis in the same spot for at least five or six years.

Note that hybrid clematis are vulnerable to wilt, while species clematis are more resistant.

Sometimes a newly transplanted clematis will collapse, leading many people to immediately suspect wilt. However, clematis doesn't like to be moved, and it could just be adjusting to its new location. If the top vine dies, don't panic—wait to see if new shoots come up. If the new shoots die, too, you've got clematis wilt; if not, it was just a matter of acclimatizing to the new locale.

Clematis ❧ hybrid clematis 'Piilu'

Are any clematis species native to Canada?

Lois ❖ Yes. Native clematis species include *Clematis occidentalis*, *Clematis ligusticifolia,* and *Clematis hirsutissima*.

Is there a fragrant clematis?

Lois ❖ Don't plant clematis for fragrance, because most varieties don't have any. Some scented clematis varieties include *Clematis heracleifolia*, 'China Purple,' *Clematis recta,* and *Clematis recta purpurea*.

Do any clematis vines tolerate shade?

Lois ❖ All clematis vines prefer full sun to partial shade. Plant them only in spots that receive at least a few hours of intense sunlight every day. Big petal clematis (*Clematis macropetala*), alpine clematis (*Clematis alpinus*), and yellow bell clematis (*Clematis tangutica*) can get by with less sun than other varieties.

How do I plant clematis?

Lois ❖ Choose a site with lots of room. Look for a spot that gets five or more hours of direct sunlight each day, but preferably one that is partly shaded during afternoon heat.

Jim ❖ Plant clematis only in rich, well-composted, pliable soil. It will not survive in heavy clay soil.

Dig a 60 cm by 60 cm hole for the plant. Plant the crown 2 cm below the soil surface and fill the hole with rich, well-drained soil. Clematis likes having cool roots, so mulch the area around the base with moss or bark chips, or plant groundcover plants.

How do I prune clematis?

Lois ❖ With alpine, big petal, or yellow bell clematis vines, prune off only dead or broken branches.

Many people cut back viticella and hybrid clematis vines in the fall, to 15-30 cm above soil level. Instead, protect the plants over the winter and prune them in the spring. To do this, gently remove the vines from their supports in late fall, and lay them stretched out on the ground. A few weeks before the soil freezes, water the roots heavily. Once the ground begins to freeze, cover the vines with 15-25 cm of dry peat moss. Uncover the vines in the spring and cut them back to the uppermost new growth.

Clematis ❧ hybrid clematis 'Duchess of Edinburgh'

I want to divide a 15-year-old Jackmanii clematis. What should I do?

Lois ❖ Don't even try. It's very difficult to successfully divide any variety of clematis. You'll end up killing your plant. Like any other living thing, every clematis has a finite lifespan. Fifteen years is about the upper limit for a Jackmanii.

Can I grow clematis in a hot, dry location? I know the roots need to be cool, but can I plant perennials in front of it?

Lois ❖ Provided you give them plenty of moisture and protect their roots from heat, clematis will do well in a hot spot.

Jim ❖ If you decide to shade the roots with other perennials, remember that these plants will compete for moisture and nutrients. You'll need to water and fertilize more often. Extra winter protection is a good idea too.

Should I pinch the shoots on a clematis to make it spread?

Lois ❖ Yes. When you pinch the growing tip of a clematis, it branches out more. Depending on the species, this might also delay flowering, but I still recommend it.

When can I transplant an established clematis?

Lois ❖ Never! Older clematis plants usually don't survive transplanting. They don't like being transplanted even when they're young. If you transplant a young clematis, you may find that it takes a year or two to fully recover.

If you absolutely must try to move a clematis, do it in the spring. The plant will suffer less stress if it has fewer leaves, and if the air and soil are cool.

Columbine

What's eating my columbine foliage?

Jim ❖ This is most likely the columbine skipper (*Erynnis lucilius*), a greenish caterpillar, 6–9 cm long, with a black head. Columbine skippers feed exclusively on columbines. They chew holes in the leaves, and also roll the leaves up. To treat, use rotenone or Sevin spray.

Another possible culprit is the columbine leaf miner (*Phytomyza aquilegivora*). Leaf miners tunnel between the layers of a leaf, leaving raised, winding patterns on the leaf surface. To treat your plant, simply pick off and destroy all infected leaves.

Aquilegia sp. ❧ columbine 'Songbird Cardinal'

Hemerocallis ❧ daylily 'Chicago Fire'

Daylily

Why won't my daylily bloom?

Lois ❖ Daylilies need six hours of direct sunlight every day; otherwise they bloom a lot less.

Your daylilies also won't bloom in the first year if they were too small when transplanted. When shopping for daylilies, choose plants that have been overwintered in pots and grown on in the spring prior to sale.

My mother grew daylilies 30 years ago and she never had big blossoms like mine. Why?

Jim ❖ Thanks to hybridization, daylilies have undergone a major transformation in recent years. They're available in a much wider range of colours, and they produce larger and more abundant flowers.

Edelweiss

I am looking for that Austrian or Swiss Alps flower. Can you help?

Lois ❖ Edelweiss (*Leontopodium alpinum*) is a small, rock garden plant about 20 cm tall. Its stems are covered with grey hair.

Fern

What are those brown spots on the undersides of the leaves on my fern?

Jim ❖ Those brown spots are the fern's reproductive structures. These spots, which are properly called sori, contain clusters of fern spores.

What species of fern is the fiddlehead that you can eat?

Lois ❖ Fiddleheads are the young shoots of the ostrich fern (*Matteuccia struthiopteris*). When an ostrich fern shoot first emerges, it forms a tight spiral, like the head of a fiddle. Fiddleheads are delicious steamed, simmered, or even raw.

Geranium endressi ❧ Endre's cranesbill

Jim ❖ Some ferns are considered toxic, but that's certainly not the case with fiddleheads. (Just make *sure* that what you're eating is a fiddlehead!)

Timing is key when harvesting fiddleheads. You've got to pick them when they're less than 15 cm long—otherwise, they begin to unfurl into fronds.

Remember that newly planted ostrich ferns need time to become established. Don't pick any fiddleheads the first year after planting your fern, and harvest only sparingly for the first few years to allow the plant to develop.

Geraniums

Are there perennial geraniums?

Lois ❖ Yes. Cranesbill is the common name for perennial geraniums.
- *Geranium cinereum* – grey-leaf cranesbill
- *Geranium endressii* – Endre's cranesbill
- *Geranium macrorrhizum* – bigroot cranesbill
- *Geranium psilostemon* – Armenian cranesbill
- *Geranium sanguineum* – blood-red cranesbill

Jim ❖ Note that perennial geraniums don't look very much like the more familiar annual geraniums. The flowers of perennial geraniums appear singly; they don't form the large, spherical heads of annual geraniums. Also, the blooming periods aren't the same.

Goutweed

How do I get rid of goutweed?

Jim ❖ We hear this question a lot! The very features that make this plant popular—its hardiness, its vigourous growth habits, its adaptability—also make it virtually impossible to kill. Glyphosate herbicides (such as Roundup) can eliminate goutweed, but you'll have to be persistent. Apply it in warm, calm weather when the goutweed is growing vigorously. After a few weeks, apply it again to any plants that have survived. You may have to continue doing this for an entire season, or for several years if the patch is well established.

Plant goutweed only in isolated areas, or confine it by installing an underground barrier to a minimum depth of 45 cm.

On the bright side, if you can't get rid of your goutweed, you can always eat it! (See Chapter 5.)

Grasses

Do any ornamental grasses flower?

Lois ❖ All ornamental grasses flower. People don't always recognize those feathery spikes as flowers, but that's what they are. Some varieties, such as pampas grass and pennisetum sp., produce very showy flowers. Others have less-conspicuous flowering habits.

Jim ❖ Ornamental grasses are wind pollinated. They don't produce brilliantly coloured flowers because they don't have to attract pollinating insects. Nevertheless, the tufted, feathery flowers on some varieties can be very attractive.

Some clumping grasses

blue fescue
blue oat grass
feather reed grass
hair grass

Some spreading grasses

bulbous oat grass
maiden grass
ribbon grass
sedges

Carex elata ❧ Bowles golden sedge 'Aurea'

Calamagrostis x *acutiflora* ❧ feather reed grass 'Overdam'

Hollyhock

What are those red spots on the undersides of my hollyhock leaves?

Jim ❖ They're called pustules. Pustules contain spores of a serious disease called rust (*Puccinia malvaccarum*), which generally attacks species of the mallow family (including hollyhocks). Each pustule disperses thousands of rust spores during the summer, infecting new hollyhocks. If the problem is confined to a few leaves, cut them off and destroy them—don't put them in the compost pile.

If you have had problems with rust in the past, you should consider applying a preventive spray of wettable sulphur. You may need to spray two to three times per week.

Hops

How can I tell male and female hops apart?

Jim ❖ The plants look the same until they bloom. Hops are dioecious, which means that they produce male and female flowers on separate plants. Male hops plants produce small greenish flowers in clusters while the female plants produce the "hops" when the vines are a couple of years old. The female flowers are also more decorative than the male flowers. Most garden centres don't differentiate between male and female plants, since they're impossible to tell apart.

If you want to make your own beer, buy the ingredients from a beer store. It's far less frustrating than buying a bunch of hops plants and hoping you'll get the right combination—not to mention the number of hops you'd require!

Hosta

Which are the largest species of hostas?

Jim ❖ The 'Blue Mammoth' hosta has been known to grow over 2 metres high and wide in Minnesota, and also grows to an impressive size farther north.

Here are some other very large hostas:
- Sum & Substance
- Big Daddy
- Frances Williams
- Sieboldiana
- Sieboldiana Elegans

Which hosta has the most fragrant blooms?

Lois ❖ The white flowers of *Hosta plantaginea* (fragrant hosta) give off a lovely fragrance when they open in the evenings. 'So Sweet' has an intense gardenia-like scent. 'Royal Standard' is both hardy and pleasantly fragrant.

Why are my hostas so slow to come up in spring?

Jim ❖ That's just the way hostas are. Some perennials, like the prairie crocus, show up as soon as the temperatures get a few degrees above freezing. Hostas, on the other hand, won't appear until temperatures hit the mid to high teens (Celsius).

Humulus lupulus ❧ hops

Why aren't my blue hostas very blue?

Jim ❖ Heat and excessive sun can fade hostas. You must grow hostas in shade for the largest leaves and best colour. It's also possible your hostas need more attention (watering, weeding, and fertilizing).

Is there a slug-resistant hosta?

Lois ❖ Try abiqua drinking gourd, or any other hosta with coarse, rubbery leaves. Slugs greatly prefer soft, tender foliage.

Hosta ❧ hosta 'Love Pat'

I planted my hostas in the sun and they are dying. Why?

Lois ❖ Hostas are shade perennials and can't survive in full sun. They grow well in morning sun (until about 10 or 11 am), but fade and burn in direct afternoon sun.

Jim ❖ Hostas are adapted to grow in the shade. Their thin, broad leaves are perfect for capturing scarce light, but also make the plants vulnerable if they're exposed to intense sunlight.

My neighbour's hostas grow in a sunny spot, but mine fade in the sun. Why is this?

Lois ❖ Yellow-leafed hosta varieties, such as 'Sun Power' and 'Sum and Substance' can tolerate much more sun than most. All hostas, however, prefer full to part shade. They tolerate morning or evening sun, but if they get too much afternoon sun, they fade or burn.

Jim ❖ In general, even an hour or two of direct sunlight in the mid afternoon can severely injure hostas. The sun's ultraviolet radiation peaks each day between 11 am and 3 pm. At the same time, the air temperature rises during the course of the day. When you expose hostas to this combination of intense sunlight and warm temperatures, their leaves quickly overheat. I would guess that your neighbour's "sunny spot" is shaded during the afternoon.

Iris

Why won't my iris bloom?

Lois ❖ Irises that are planted too deeply produce leaves but no blooms. The rhizomes should be barely covered with soil.

Jim ❖ If you've got an old clump that hasn't been divided for several years, dividing it might solve the problem. There's also the chance that your iris was too young to produce flowers when transplanted, or that it isn't getting enough sunlight.

What is the difference between Japanese and German irises?

Jim ❖ The Japanese iris (*Iris ensata*) is a woodland iris that does well in moist soils (even ponds!) and part sun. It likes acid soil and tolerates full sun if you keep the soil constantly moist. The German iris (*Iris germanica*) produces larger, brightly coloured, fragrant flowers. It grows best in full sun and tolerates dry soil.

Why is my bearded iris rotting at the base?

Lois ❖ You may have planted it too deep. You should leave the rhizome barely exposed, particularly in heavy soils. Your iris may also rot if you keep it too wet or if your soil drains poorly.

Which iris can I plant around a pond?

Jim ❖ Try Japanese iris (*Iris ensata*), yellow flag iris (*I. pseudacorus*), blue flag iris (*I. versicolor*), or Siberian iris (*I. sibirica*).

Iris germanica ❧ bearded iris 'Breakers'

Lavender

My lavender died over the winter. How can I prevent this next time?

Jim ❖ Lavender is a zone 5 plant, meaning that it requires extra winter protection in regions with harsh winters. Treat it as you would a tender rose—mulch it with a thick layer of peat moss in the fall and (if you can) shovel some extra snow onto it during the winter for extra insulation.

Lavender likes a drier soil. It's much more susceptible to winter injury if it's grown in wet, heavy soil.

Ligularia (Rayflower)

Why does my ligularia wilt in the middle of the day and perk up at night?

Lois ❖ Ligularia doesn't like heat or hot, bright sun. When the plant suffers heat stress, the leaves wilt and then recover in the evening.

Grow ligularia only in cool, moist areas. They love sites around ponds or stream banks, or anywhere where their roots are consistently moist.

Lily

Will lilies tolerate any shade? Do any lilies rebloom?

Lois ❖ Martagon lilies grow best in partial shade. Asiatics do best in southern or western exposures. Most lilies bloom only once per season, although some daylilies will rebloom.

I want nice long stems on my lilies for cutting. Can I cut them off right at the ground?

Lois ❖ Hybrid (Asiatic and Oriental) lilies do have beautiful stems, often two or three feet long. You can cut very long stems, but leave at least 30 cm of foliage behind so that the plant can produce energy for the winter.

What are the differences between Oriental (*Lilium orientale*) and Asiatic lilies (*Lilium spp.*)?

Jim ❖ Oriental lilies produce larger, more fragrant blooms, but are less hardy—you should either mulch them well, plant them against a house wall, or dig them up each fall and store them indoors.

Asiatic lilies produce smaller, more numerous flowers per stem and are much more cold tolerant.

Are stargazer lilies hardy in zone 3?

Lois ❖ Stargazer lilies are Oriental, which means that they are not really hardy in zone 3. They can survive if you give them a lot of winter protection. Plant them against a house wall or foundation, and give them a good protective cover of mulch before winter comes.

Lilium ❦ Asiatic lily 'Delta'

Lilium ❦ Oriental lily 'Stargazer'

Can I plant the little bulb things that form on lily stems?

Lois ❖ Yes, you can plant them. It may take a couple of years, though, be-fore they produce flowers of their own. They need to reach a minimum size before they have enough energy to support flower production.

Jim ❖ All bulb-producing species of plants produce these "little bulb things," properly called bulbils.

On lilies, you can find bulbils in the leaf axils above ground and below ground (these are called bulblets).

I bought a lily a week ago and now the flowers have fallen off. Why don't I have any more blooms?

Lois ❖ Lilies have a short but glorious blooming period that usually lasts about 2 to 4 weeks. It can be shortened by warmer weather or lengthened by cooler temperatures. The lily you purchased was probably nearing the end of its blooming period. If you plant early- and late-blooming varieties together, you can create a lily bed that blooms continuously for up to six weeks.

When do you dig up Oriental lily bulbs?

Lois ❖ Dig up your bulbs in the late fall. Leave them in the ground as long as possible, right up until the ground freezes. In the meantime, there's no better place to store your bulbs.

Zantedeschia ❧ calla 'Black Magic'

How do I overwinter my calla lilies? I have them in an oak barrel—is it okay to put them in the ground like my other lilies?

Jim ❖ Unless you're lucky enough to live in a zone 9 or 10 region, you can't leave your callas in the ground over the winter. Treat them as you would gladioli. Dig the bulbs up after the first frost, let them dry, clean off the dirt, and store them in vermiculite at about 4 to 10°C

(Purple) Loosestrife

Why isn't lythrum (purple loosestrife) available any more?

Jim ❖ It is illegal to sell or even possess loosestrife in most provinces and states in North America. A beautiful, tough plant with long purple spikes, loosestrife was a popular garden perennial for decades. Unfortunately, it's highly invasive—so invasive, in fact, that it has taken over large areas of wetlands in North America, out-competing and eliminating native plants. A single loosestrife plant can produce up to three million seeds in a single year, with a very high germination rate. To combat its spread, loosestrife was declared a noxious weed.

In an attempt to salvage the plant for home gardens, plant breeders produced a few cultivars that were thought to be sterile and thus incapable of spreading in the wild. Unfortunately, these cultivars proved capable of cross-pollinating with wild loosestrife. Eventually, all varieties were banned.

If you have purple loosestrife, check with your local garden centre to see if it is participating in the special program that allows you to turn in your loosestrife for a free plant.

Armeria maritima ❧ sea pink 'Pride of Dusseldorf'

Lupinus x *hybrida* ❧ lupine

Lupine

Why do I constantly lose my lupines even though they are winter hardy?

Lois ❖ Lupines are short-lived perennials, seldom surviving beyond three winters. They hate hot, humid summers and wet winters. They also prefer alkaline soils, relatively low in nutrients, they deplete rich soils quickly. If you love lupines, you simply have to be prepared to replace them regularly.

Lupines do self-sow readily, although people often mistake the seedlings for weeds. Leave the flowers on the plants, so they'll have the chance to produce seed.

Peony

How long does it take for peonies to bloom?

Lois ❖ Potted peonies bloom the first year, provided the root system is large enough. When you buy roots, make sure they have three to five eyes—that way, you'll likely get blooms the first year. Tree peonies can take two or three years before they begin to bloom. Roots develop the first summer and shoots develop the second spring.

What are the differences among types of peonies?

Lois ❖ There are dozens of different species peonies and hybrid peonies, in a wide assortment of colours, sizes, and growth habits. Species peonies are the earliest bloomers, while hybrids tend to be slower to reveal themselves.

Jim ❖ Fernleaf peony (*P. tenuifolia*), one of many species peonies, produces fern-like foliage and dies to the ground in winter (that is, it's herbaceous). Hybrid peonies (*P. lactiflora* or *P. officinalis*) are large plants (1 m high, 1 m across) that die to the ground in winter and generally have smaller flowers. They are divided into 3 main categories—early hybrids, Japanese, and doubles—and generally bloom in that order. The tree peony (*Paeonia suffructicosa*) has woody stems and does not die back to the ground in winter; its big flowers are usually semi-double. The Itoh peony (*P.* x *itoh*) is a cross between a hybrid and a tree peony; it retains many of the tree peony's characteristics with small to medium-sized flowers which are mostly semi-double. In colder climates, the Itoh may die back in the winter, but it will grow back from the ground.

Paeonia x *itoh* ❧ Itoh peony 'Yellow Crown'

Paeonia ❦ early hybrid peony 'Coral Charm'

Can I cut my peony right down after it has finished blooming?

Jim ❖ Don't do that. In the months after your peonies stop blooming, their leaves continue to produce food for the storage roots. If you don't allow your peonies to complete this part of their cycle, they'll be less vigorous next year and produce fewer blooms.

Do ants harm peonies?

Jim ❖ No. Ants love to feed on the sugars exuded by the flower buds, but they don't harm peonies. The ants usually show up just before the buds start to open, which likely led to the popular myth that peonies need ants in order to bloom.

Why won't my peonies bloom?

Jim ❖ Here are the most likely possible explanations.
- They're planted too deep. Even 8 cm of soil over the "eyes" can be too deep.
- The roots were recently transplanted. It can take several years before divided peonies bloom profusely.
- The roots are too small.
- The roots have no "eyes" or have only damaged ones.
- They're not getting enough sun. Peonies need at least six hours of sunlight each day to bloom well.
- Grey mould (botrytis) attacked the petioles (flower stems) before the blossoms formed.
- The weather was too dry when the flowers buds were forming.
- The soil isn't sufficiently fertile.

How deep should I plant my peony? Why?

Lois ❖ Plant peonies with only 3–5 cm of soil over the "eyes." If you bury peonies deeper than 8 cm, they may not bloom.

My peonies turn brown and woody at the base and then die. Why?

Jim ❖ Assuming they're not tree peonies (which have woody stems), the likely culprit is a fungal disease called *Sclerotinia sclerotiorum*. Fungicides are ineffective against these infections. Your best solution is to purchase new, healthy peonies.

Why did my peony flowers change colours?

Jim ❖ Temperature can greatly affect bloom colour. Flowers tend to be brighter in cooler weather and paler in hot. Petals also fade as flowers age.

My fernleaf peony looked nice when I planted it this spring, but now it is turning yellow and dying. Why?

Jim ❖ Newly planted fernleaf peonies always go dormant in early summer. Some plants do this to cope with the summer heat. The plant isn't injured, however—the dormancy is just part of its natural growth cycle. It will emerge again next spring.

Paeonia tenuifolia ❧ double fernleaf peony

I can't get my tree peony to bloom. It's 5 years old. Why?

Jim ❖ Tree peonies bloom only on old wood, and they aren't as hardy as other peonies. If your plant continually dies back to the ground in winter, you'll never see flowers because old wood never gets a chance to form. Be sure to mulch your tree peonies in the fall to prevent winter injury.

Poppy

Do Himalayan poppies set seed?

Jim ❖ They do, but this doesn't make them a good bet for home seeding! Himalayan poppy seeds require cool temperatures (10°C) to germinate. Even then, they germinate sporadically—taking anywhere from three weeks to two years!

Papaver orientale ❧ Oriental poppy 'Turkenlouis'

What special care do Himalayan poppies need?

Lois ❖ Very little! They're generally very easy to care for and a delight to grow with their wonderful blue colour. They prefer cool, bright summers, and perform poorly in hot, humid climates.

Location is the key to success. Plant them in a shady spot, in slightly acidic soil. Give them plenty of leaf mould or peat moss. Over the growing season, keep them moist and undisturbed.

Because these large plants tend to go dormant in the summer heat, you'll want to have another plant ready to fill in the space later in the season.

Jim ❖ We've had great difficulty shipping poppies, because they hate being boxed and transported for any length of time.

Meconopsis grandis ❧ Himalayan poppy

Perovskia atriplicifolia ❧ Russian sage

Rhubarb

What's the difference between ornamental rhubarb and edible rhubarb?

Jim ❖ Edible rhubarb (*Rheum rhubarbarum*) and ornamental rhubarb (*Rheum palmatum*) are two separate species. Ornamental rhubarb tastes awful and is also poisonous. If you're planning to bake a pie, you'll definitely want to stick with regular rhubarb!

Russian Sage

Do you cut back Russian sage in the spring or does it grow back on old wood?

Lois ❖ Russian sage (*Perovskia atriplicifolia*) does indeed grow back on its woody stems, so you shouldn't cut it back in the fall. In the spring, cut it back to the point just above the new leaves.

Shasta Daisy

What is the difference between ox-eye daisies and Shasta daisies?

Jim ❖ Ox-eye daisy (*Chrysanthemum leucanthemum*) is the wild daisy you often see growing in ditches and vacant lots. Because it's prolific, invasive, and very hardy, ox-eye daisy is considered a noxious weed in many areas.

Shasta daisies (*Leucanthemum superbum*) are the classic "She loves me, she loves me not" flower found so often in perennial gardens. While they aren't nearly as aggressive as ox-eye daisies, you should remove spent flower heads before they set seed, unless you don't mind having new daisies sprouting throughout your garden.

Leucanthemum x *superbum* ❦ Shasta daisy 'Alaska'

Erigeron sp. ❧ showy daisy 'Foerster's Liebling'

Showy Daisy

Why do you call a plant showy daisy while I know it as fleabane?

Lois ❖ I could give you dozens of similar examples! Many perennials have two or more common names. That's why it's so often handy knowing a plant's Latin name—every plant has only one of those!

Jim ❖ Many traditional perennial names sound less than appealing (fleabane is a perfect example!). In some cases, the unflattering common names are being gradually displaced by more picturesque names (e.g., fleabane—showy daisy, dead nettle—white archangel), and in other cases the plants are becoming more commonly known by their Latin names (e.g., lungwort—*Pulmonaria*).

Silver Mound

I know silver mound should form a nice, round clump, but mine gets all straggly. Why?

Lois ❖ In hot, humid weather, silver mound (*Artemisia schmidtiana*) often opens in the centre and then slumps down. Too much moisture or too much nitrogen (manure, compost, or fertilizer) can also cause it to go straggly and limp. Be careful not to overwater or overfertilize.

Statice

What is the difference between sea lavender and German statice?

Lois ❖ These two lovely statice species are closely related—they're both members of the *Limonium* genus. Sea lavender (*Limonium platyphyllum*) produces loose, airy clusters of flowers, similar to baby's breath. German statice (*Limonium tataricum*) produces tighter, coarser flower clusters.

Valerian

I have a valerian growing in my garden where I didn't plant it. Why?

Lois ❖ Valerians produce lots of seeds, which spread easily and germinate readily. I expect there's a valerian growing nearby, either in your garden or your neighbour's.

Virginia Creeper

Which surfaces will Virginia creeper cling to on its own?

Lois ❖ Some varieties won't cling to any surface on their own. The 'Engelmannii' variety, however, will cling to almost any surface. About the only surface they have trouble with is vinyl or metal siding. I've even seen them wound around an old pitch fork left against the side of a barn!

Jim ❖ Virginia creeper 'Engelmanni' and Boston ivy have tendrils that form adhesive pads at their tips. These adhesive pads attach to almost any surface and are difficult to dislodge.

Artemisia schmidtiana nana ❧ silver mound

Which Virginia creeper species turns red in the fall?

Lois ❖ All the Virginia creepers turn red, as long as the weather in August and September is generally sunny and warm during the day and cooler at night. If the fall is too short or too cold, they won't turn red. This happens from time to time where I live.

Jim ❖ As with other plants that turn red in the fall, Virginia creeper leaves contain large levels of chemicals called flavonoids. As the green chlorophyll in the leaves breaks down in the fall, the flavonoids are gradually converted into anthocyanins, which turn the leaves red.

What are the bugs attacking my Virginia creeper and what can I do about them?

Jim ❖ Virginia creepers are highly vulnerable to the grape leafhopper. This small insect reproduces rapidly in warm weather. When disturbed, the leafhoppers jump up en masse and appear to be flying. Like mosquitoes sucking blood, they pierce plant tissues and draw sap directly from the plant. They leave white blotches on the leaves where they have been feeding.

You're best off if you can catch the problem early in the season, before the leafhopper population explodes.

Yarrow

Why does my yarrow fall over and form large, messy mats?

Lois ❖ Yarrow (*Achillea*) can be a very aggressive plant, depending on the species, and tends to become overgrown. When the blooms fade, cut the plants back to encourage renewed growth and flowering. If you're careful not to give them too much fertilizer, the problem won't be as bad.

Jim ❖ Several factors, alone or in combination, can cause yarrow to lodge (fall over).

- Inadequate light: yarrow prefers full sun, and becomes weak and floppy in shade.
- Overly rich soil: yarrow becomes weak and overgrown if it receives too much nitrogen.
- Overwatering.
- Crowding: your plants may be too close together
- Warm night temperatures: unless the nights are cool, yarrow doesn't acquire enough carbohydrates to strengthen the stem.

Parthenocissus quinquefolia ❧ Virginia creeper 'Star Showers'

My yarrow attracts green bottle flies. I've also noticed that the flowers stink. Is there a connection?

Jim ❖ Different plant species attract different pollinators. Some flowers give off scents reminiscent of dead animal matter and manure, specifically to attract flies. That's why the flies love the smell of your yarrow, while you can't stand it.

On the bright side, according to English folklore, yarrow repels troublesome fairies. So, although you may have a few more flies in your garden, the yarrow should keep your fairy problems to a minimum!

Achillea tomentosa ❧ yarrow

Afterword
by Jim Hole

I love to learn, and preparing this book on perennials gave me plenty
of opportunities to do just that. I've always been more interested in the
mechanics of the real world than the imaginary narratives of novels or
films, and working with perennials provides plenty of drama. Don't get
me wrong—I love a good story as much as the next guy, but a chance to
learn about the inner workings of nature holds more appeal for me. Sometimes Mom describes me as a kind of walking gardening encyclopedia, but
the truth is, as you might have guessed, a little more complex. Although my
sister-in-law calls me "Mr. Science," I don't pretend to know everything.
But it bugs me if someone asks me a question and I don't know the answer.
More often than not, the solution isn't in my head; I have to pull out a text-
book or consult a specialist. Over the years I've naturally assimilated plenty
of gardening knowledge because of that inability to let a question go without a response. Putting together these books has been very fulfilling for
that reason: your questions gave me the chance to do some extra research
and discover a number of things I wasn't previously aware of.

I've been asked what my favourite perennial is, but this group of plants is so
incredibly diverse that it's difficult to choose one over another. That diversity
makes perennials intensely intriguing: there's always something new to discover, aesthetically and scientifically. Obviously, this is by no means the final
chapter on these fascinating plants.

So Ask Us Some Questions...

We plan to update all of the Question and Answer books periodically. If you
have a gardening question that's been troubling you, write to us! While we
can't answer your inquiries individually, your question may appear in future
Q&A books—along with the answer, naturally. And don't ever think that a
question is "dumb" or "too simple." Odds are that any mysteries you face are
shared by countless other gardeners.

Send your questions to:
Hole's Q&A Questions
101 Bellerose Drive
St. Albert, AB T8N 8N8
CANADA

You can also send us e-mail at **yourquestions@enjoygardening.com**
or visit us at **www.enjoygardening.com**

index

slug, 85
snow, 29, 30, 59, 76
soil, 18, 21, 26, 62, 69, 89, 95
   acidic, 26
   alkaline, 22
   clay, 23
soil test, 20
space, 52
spring, 58, 59, 71, 75
Sulphur, 20
sulphur, 21, 23, 25
sun, 28, 30, 63, 95

T

thrips, 91
tissue cultures, 56
topsoil, 19, 22, 68
transplant, 49, 50, 52, 60, 63, 108
transplants, 60

U

underwatering, 62

V

varieties, choosing, 28

W

water, 60, 61, 62, 74, 88, 90
waterlogged, 19, 88
weeds, 19, 35, 67, 68, 69, 132
wildlife, 88
wilt, clematis, 104
wilting, 90
winter, 30, 45, 70, 71, 96, 119
winters, 19
woodland, 36
worm, green, 84

Z

zinc, 21
zone, 29, 75

Question: *Who is Lois Hole?*

Answer ❖ The author of eight best-selling books, Lois Hole provides practical advice that's both accessible and essential. Her knowledge springs from years of hands-on experience as a gardener and greenhouse operator. She's shared that knowledge for years through her books, her popular newspaper columns, hundreds of gardening talks all over the continent, and dozens of radio and television appearances. Never afraid to get her hands dirty, Lois answers all of your gardening questions with warmth and wit.

Question: *Who is Jim Hole?*

Answer ❖ Inheriting his mother's love of horticulture, Jim Hole grew up in the garden. After spending his formative years on the Hole farm in St. Albert, Jim attended the University of Alberta, expanding his knowledge and earning a Bachelor of Science in Agriculture. Jim appears regularly on radio and television call-in shows to share what he's learned, and writes a weekly gardening column for the *Edmonton Journal* and the *National Post*. Jim's focus is on the science behind the garden—he explains what makes plants tick in a clear and concise style, without losing sight of the beauty and wonder that makes gardening worthwhile.

Lois and Jim have worked together for years on books, newspaper articles, and gardening talks. Working with family members Ted Hole, Bill Hole, and Valerie Hole, Lois and Jim helped to create Hole's, a greenhouse and garden centre that ranks among the largest retail gardening operations in Canada. The books in the *Q&A* series mark Lois and Jim's first official collaboration.

"One last question..."

How did a Q&A book about perennials come about?

Perennials: Practical Advice and the Science Behind It is the final volume in the first trilogy of *Q&A* titles. *Perennials*, combined with *Bedding Plants* and *Roses*, answers the majority of questions we collected during the past year.

Finding and providing the answers required the efforts of dozens of people. Our greenhouse and perennials staff collected questions throughout the spring and summer, then added the questions they had on file as well as everything they remembered. **Liz Grieve** was hired to do a rough sort of the questions, selecting the questions that would form the basis of this book.

As was the case for the first *Q&A* volumes, **Jim Hole** sat down with **Julia Mamolo** to complete the first rough answers. These were passed on to **Lois Hole** for her answers and to the rest of the family for a first kick at refinement. Meanwhile, Jim hit the books and started to dig for the science.

As the rough text began to take shape, **Scott Rollans**, the series editor, started to fit the text to the shape and style of the new series. The text was revised and formatted to fit its final form. As the information poured in and the questions and answers were refined, **Earl Woods** polished sections, filled in blank spaces, and worked with Lois to prepare the introductions.

The text then went back to Jim and our resident perennials experts, **Bob Stadnyk** and **Jan Goodall**. Designer **Greg Brown** began work fitting the new text into the established design. He worked with **Christina McDonald** to find images from Hole's photo library to enhance the overall presentation.

As the final revisions came in, production assistant **Stephan Messenger** made the changes to the layout, while **Leslie Vermeer** undertook final edits and proofing. The completed book file was delivered to Elite Lithography for output to final film. After the film and proofs were checked, it was sent to Friesens to produce the book you now hold.

$$H$$

Publication Director ❖ Bruce Timothy Keith

Series Editor ❖ Scott Rollans

Editorial Assistant ❖ Julia Mamolo

Writing & Research ❖ Earl J. Woods

Proofing & Editorial ❖ Leslie Vermeer

Book Design & Production ❖ Gregory Brown

Production Assistant ❖ Stephan Messenger